THE HAMMARSKJÖLD FORUMS

**Case Studies
on
The Role of Law
in the
Settlement of International Disputes**

THE PANAMA CANAL

BACKGROUND PAPERS AND PROCEEDINGS
of
THE SIXTH HAMMARSKJÖLD FORUM

RICHARD R. BAXTER
and
DORIS CARROLL
Authors of the Working Paper

LYMAN M. TONDEL, Jr.
Editor

Published for
THE ASSOCIATION OF THE BAR OF THE CITY OF NEW YORK
by
OCEANA PUBLICATIONS, INC.
DOBBS FERRY, N. Y.
1965

Library of Congress Catalog Card Number: 65-22162

PRINTED IN THE UNITED STATES OF AMERICA

Table of Contents

Part One
THE WORKING PAPER

Part Two

A SUMMARY OF THE FORUM PROCEEDINGS

Participants: Richard Reeve Baxter, Joseph A. Califano, Jr., Joseph Simpson Farland, and Victor C. Folsom

APPENDIX

EDITOR'S FOREWORD

This is the sixth in the series of books based on the Hammarskjöld Forums that are being conducted by The Association of the Bar of the City of New York as case studies on "The Role of Law in the Settlement of International Disputes." The first five books were based on forums on The Issues in the Berlin-German Crisis; The Role of the United Nations in the Congo; The Inter-American Security System and the Cuban Crisis of October, 1962; Disarmament; and The International Position of Communist China.

In addition to distribution through usual channels, the volumes are being distributed by the Association, with the aid of a grant from the Ford Foundation, to about 1,000 selected leaders of the bar in the field of international law, teachers in related fields, and organizations interested in foreign affairs. Their reception has been excellent.

The foreword to the first four volumes recited the history and purposes of these Forums, and books, and there is no need for repetition here. We do, however, wish to renew our acknowledgement to all those who have made this series possible, including particularly James N. Rosenberg, who has supplied initiative and funds and whose 90th birthday inspired gifts totalling about $25,000 to support the continuation of this series; the Ford Foundation; the authors of the Working Papers (Professors Robert Bowie, Thomas Franck, Covey Oliver, Louis Henken and Richard Baxter, Mr. O. Edmund Clubb, Miss Doris Carroll and John Carey, Esq.); all the distinguished participants in the forums; Miss Carroll, Mr. Carey, William D. Zabel, Esq., Robert M. Pennoyer, Esq., and Isaac Shapiro, Esq. who have prepared the summaries of the discussions at the forums; and Arthur A. Charpentier, Librarian of the Association, Joseph L. Andrews, Reference Librarian, Anthony P. Grech, Assistant Reference Librarian, and their staff, who have prepared the comprehensive bibliographies for the volumes.

If the nations are to find means of peacefully solving controversies with each other, the search for such means can only be hastened by greater knowledge and understanding of what actions, ambitions, needs or ideologies have led to critical disputes; of what procedures and devices have helped solve such disputes, and what have not; of what new laws, customs, procedures and institutions are evolving in connection with efforts to solve such disputes; of the extent to which rulers have had regard for international law, or at least the pretext of legality; and of what sanctions, obligations, and other considerations have restrained them the most. Furthermore, it is important that leaders of community opinion have readily at hand authoritative information as to the facts that underlie major international disputes and the complex issues that they present; and that such leaders understand that most such issues can be fairly resolved only if there is thorough understanding of the facts and of the reasons for the varying points of view of the nations involved, and by persistent patience.

In publishing these little volumes it is intended that each provide, in brief and readable form, the essential background information on a specific controversy, together with extensive bibliographies for further study, if desired; that each alert the reader to the existing and developing law and legal institutions involved in the particular controversy; and that all who read may thereby become more aware that only by the substitution of the rule of law may war be eliminated as the ultimate means of settling international disputes.

Lyman M. Tondel, Jr.

PART ONE

THE WORKING PAPER

WORKING PAPER: THE PANAMA CANAL*

R. R. BAXTER
Professor of Law, Harvard Law School

DORIS CARROLL
of the New York and Massachusetts Bars

INTRODUCTION

On April 3, 1964 the United States and Panama formally agreed to re-establish diplomatic relations which had been severed since January 1964 when, after riots at the Canal Zone border in which 27 persons were killed, over 400 injured, and extensive property damage done, Panama recalled her Ambassador at Washington and required United States diplomatic personnel to leave Panama. In that twelve-week interval hemispheric efforts to mend the rift through use of peace-keeping machinery of the Organization of American States met with a persistent obstable—Panamanian President Chiari's insistence upon, and President Johnson's refusal to give, a prior and definite commitment that the United States would undertake to negotiate fundamental revision of the 1903 Treaty which gave the United States sovereign rights in perpetuity in the Canal Zone. The formula of accord which was at length agreed upon makes no express reference to treaty revision, but does provide for the designation of special ambassadors "with sufficient powers to seek the prompt elimination of the causes of conflict between the two countries" who are to "begin immediately the necessary procedures with the objective of reaching a just and fair agreement. . . ."

The crux of the conflict, manifested in the intricate dialogue

---

* The Authors in planning this Working Paper were aided by the wise counsel of Professor Norman J. Padelford of the Massachusetts Institute of Technology, and they acknowledge his help with warm thanks.

1

about whether there should be "discussions" or "negotiations" of differences between Panama and the United States, has been whether a new régime should be created for the Canal by a new treaty, if not now, at least in the foreseeable future. The United States position calls for a maintenance of the status quo, subject to minor adjustments; the Panamanian for major changes.

If the problem of the future of the Panama Canal is unique, the problem of Panama is not. How the demand for stability and the demand for change can be peaceably reconciled is a central problem of contemporary international relations and international law. If change is to come peacefully, the lawyer must become the architect of new institutions, a task which he cannot undertake to perform intelligently without an understanding of prior patterns and present needs. The highest creative powers of the lawyer will be called for if the legitimate demands of Panama are to be met without the loss of what is essential to the United States. The alternative to a just and viable solution can only be continuing conflict, the impact of which will be felt not only in Panama and the other American republics but throughout the world.

I. CRISIS: THE EVENTS OF JANUARY—APRIL 1964

A. *The January Riots*

The incident which touched off the three-month break in diplomatic relations was one likely to bring Panamanian nationalistic passions to a boil—passions simmering in recent years about the question whether the Panamanian flag should fly in the Canal Zone, territory within which Panama had renounced the exercise of sovereign rights, power or authority by treaty in 1903. On January 7, 1964 North American students at Balboa High School in the Canal Zone, in deliberate defiance of a 1963 agreement between the two nations that American and Panamanian flags would fly together throughout the Canal Zone wherever the United States flag was flown by civilian authorities, raised the United States flag alone in front of their school. Thereafter a group of Panamanian students entered the Canal Zone with the purpose of planting their own national flag at the school. Reports were that in an ensuing clash between students and Canal Zone police the Panamanian flag was defiled. For the next several days and nights Panamanians demonstrated at the border, their forays into the Zone repulsed by Canal Zone police and United States soldiers using tear gas. During January 9-10 when Panamanian authorities did nothing to quell sniper gunfire into the Zone, United States troops were authorized to direct bird-shot against the men firing from the Panamanian side, and trained marksmen of the Army Rifle Team performed countersniper fire. Anti-United States rioters set afire and destroyed buildings and property of Panamanians and United States nationals in the Zone and in Panama.

B. *International Peace-Keeping Efforts*

"Acts of aggression by the United States" was the reason given by Panama for breaking diplomatic relations with the United States. On January 9 President Chiari had recalled the Panaman-

3

ian Ambassador at Washington. (The American Embassy in Panama had been without an ambassador since August 1963, when Joseph S. Farland resigned from the post reportedly after a series of differences with the Department of State about American policy in Panama.) On January 10, charging that U.S. military authorities had opened an "unprovoked armed attack" against Panama's territory and its civilian population, the Panamanian Foreign Minister demanded an emergency meeting of the Council of the Organization of American States under articles 6 and 9(a) of the 1947 Rio de Janeiro Pact,[1] and the Panamanian delegate to the United Nations asked that the Security Council be convoked under articles 34 and 35 of the United Nations Charter.[2] But then President Johnson spoke to President Chiari by telephone on January 10, and the Heads of State agreed rather to use the good offices of the Inter-American Peace Committee[3] in a mutual effort to restore and maintain peace and safety in Panama and the Canal Zone and to mend the breach in relations between their two countries.

Order had been restored in Panama within five days of the first riots through action by Panamanian and American authorities. But all attempts by the five-nation[4] Peace Committee in the next three weeks to effect a resumption of diplomatic ties between the two countries foundered on the issue of commitment to treaty revision. On January 15 the Peace Committee announced that there was an agreement for the re-establishment of relations; that accord came to naught when the United States insisted it had agreed only to "discuss" questions affecting American-Panamanian affairs, while Panama maintained that the United States had undertaken to "negotiate" settlement of those questions. What had seemed at first to be merely a semantic difficulty became in the political circumstances an issue of major proportions: Presidential elections were to take place in Panama in May, and all of the candidates, even Arnulfo Arias who was the major candidate opposing President Chiari's party, espoused the popular demand for revision of the Canal Zone treaties. On January 17 Panama formally required United States diplomatic personnel and the U.S. military mission to leave Panama. In turn the United States suspended its economic aid to Panama.[5]

On January 29 Panama set in motion the collective security

4

procedures of the Rio Pact[6] by asking the Council of the Organization of American States to decide that circumstances were such as to justify convocation of the Organ of Consultation pursuant to article 6 of the treaty, which reads:

> "If the inviolability or the integrity of the territory or the sovereignty or political independence of any American State should be affected by an aggression which is not an armed attack or by an extra-continental or intra-continental conflict, or by any other fact or situation that might endanger the peace of America, the Organ of Consultation shall meet immediately in order to agree on the measures which must be taken in case of aggression to assist the victim of the aggression or, in any case, the measures which should be taken for the common defense and for the maintenance of the peace and security of the Continent."

The Organ of Consultation is composed of the foreign ministers of the American republics which have ratified the Rio Pact;[7] their convocation cannot as a practical matter be expected to be accomplished "immediately". Therefore article 12 of the Treaty permits the O.A.S. Council to act provisionally as an "organ of consultation" until the foreign ministers shall actually have met. The existence of article 12 has led to an interesting shortcut: In most of the instances in which the O.A.S. Council has found it necessary to call a meeting of the Organ of Consultation, the Council has not set an actual date for the meeting, but has itself acted provisionally as such organ, found a solution for the situation leading to the request for the meeting of American foreign ministers, and then called off the requested meeting.[8] That practice was followed in the case of Panama's request: On February 4 the O.A.S. Council heard Panama's charges of United States aggression and then resolved to constitute itself a provisional "organ of consultation." On February 7 that Organ of Consultation decided to establish a 17-nation committee (all the American republics with representatives in the Council save the United States and Panama) to investigate and mediate the Panamanian-U.S. conflict.[9] Thereupon a five-nation subcommittee composed of the representatives from Paraguay, Brazil, Costa Rica, Mexico, and Uruguay was dispatched to Panama on a week-long fact-finding mission. The subcommittee made no public report of its investigation, but there have been newspaper reports that it con-

5

cluded that the United States was not guilty of deliberate armed aggression and that there was no ground to invoke Rio Pact sanctions against her.[10]

Thereafter until April 1964 the five-nation subcommittee of the General Committee of the Organ of Consultation worked with Panamanian and U.S. representatives to draft a conciliation formula acceptable to both countries. In mid-March an end to the impasse seemed so near that the O.A.S. mediators, without waiting for formal governmental endorsements, made public an agreed-upon formula calling for the appointment of special ambassadors who would "carry out discussions and negotiations with the objective of reaching fair and just international agreement." But that accord too proved to be still-born, for the United States disagreed with the Panamanian interpretation of the formula as a firm commitment of the United States to revision of the Canal Zone treaty.

C. *The Accord of April 3, 1964*

On April 3, 1964 both countries were able at last to declare jointly that an agreement had been reached for the resumption of diplomatic relations and for further conferences. Their joint declaration read:

> "In accordance with the friendly declarations of the Presidents of the United States of America and of the Republic of Panama of the 21st and 24th of March, 1964, respectively, annexed hereto, which are in agreement in a sincere desire to resolve favorably all the differences between the two countries;
> "Meeting under the chairmanship of the President of the Council and recognizing the important cooperation offered by the Organization of American States through the Inter-American Peace Committee and the delegation of the General Committee of the Organ of Consultation, the representatives of both Governments have agreed:
> "1. To re-establish diplomatic relations.
> "2. To designate without delay special Ambassadors with sufficient powers to seek the prompt elimination of the causes of conflict between the two countries, without limitations or preconditions of any kind.
> "3. That therefore, the Ambassadors designated will began immediately the necessary procedures with the objective of reaching a just and fair agreement which would be subject to the constitutional process of each country." [11]

6

Both nations did move without delay to resume relations and to appoint ambassadors. Sr. Miguel J. Moreno, Jr., who had taken over as Panama's delegate to the O.A.S. and was his country's active negotiator throughout the crisis, was named to be the new Panamanian Ambassador at Washington. (Ambassador Moreno, a presidential candidate in the May 1964 elections in Panama, participated in the negotiation of the Treaty of 1955 with the United States.) Sr. Jorge Iluecas, a law professor and newspaper publisher, will be one of Panama's negotiators in the forthcoming talks. For the United States, Mr. Jack Hood Vaughn, lately Latin-American director for the Peace Corps and formerly a member of the U.S. economic aid mission to Panama, has been appointed Ambassador to Panama, and Mr. Robert B. Anderson has been chosen as chief United States negotiator in the conferences contemplated in the join declaration of April 3.

II. BACKGROUND OF THE DISPUTE

A. *Commercial and Strategic Value of the Panama Canal*

In 1523 the desirability of a direct all-water route from Cadiz to the riches of Cathay prompted Charles V of Spain to initiate the first studies for a canal to be cut through the isthmus which links North and South America.[12] The advantages for sea-going commerce of such a joining of Atlantic and Pacific Oceans continued to engage the interest of major maritime powers through the next centuries. By the nineteenth century it was clear that to serve world commerce and inter-oceanic waterway would surely be built through some Central American region, probably by a private company privately financed. By the end of the nineteenth century it was manifest that, for imperative strategic as well as commercial reasons, the United States alone would construct and operate that canal. Two resolutions of the Senate of the United States exemplify the shift in American attitude over time: In 1835 the Senate urged the President to negotiate with various nations for the protection of such individuals or companies as might undertake the construction of a trans-isthmian canal, as well as for securing free and equal rights of navigation to all nations; [13] in 1889, when following the financial collapse of De Lesseps' French canal company the French Government proposed to guarantee the company's bonds, a resolution was introduced in the Senate that:

> "the Government of the United States will look with serious concern and disapproval upon any connection of any European government with the construction or control of any ship-canal across the Isthmus of Darien or across Central America, and must regard any such connection or control as injurious to the just rights and interests of the United States and as a menace to their welfare." [14]

The dominating considerations which impelled the United States itself to undertake construction and control of the isthmian canal were strategic and military. A number of events occurring at the turn of the century—among them the ninety-day race of the U.S. cruiser *Oregon* around the Horn to participate in the battle of Santiago de Cuba during the Spanish-American War; the American conquest of the Philippines and the annexation of the Hawaiian Islands, bringing new U.S. opportunities and responsibilities in the Pacific; and foreign adventures in China—focussed American attention upon the vital necessity of having its naval forces readily available for duty in the Atlantic and Pacific Oceans and the Caribbean Sea. A surging expansion of U.S. foreign trade quickening in that era undoubtedly contributed a complementary commercial motive for canal construction, but from the outset the Panama Canal had for the United States primarily a military aspect.

Through two world wars the Panama Canal has been for the United States an essential instrument of national defense, used for the flexible deployment of military forces to meet a threat in either ocean and for the accelerated transport of vital raw materials and military supplies. The primary role of the Canal in World War I was logistic, for during that war naval activity was centered chiefly in the Atlantic. But in World War II the ability of America's warships to rendezvous anywhere in the world in three weeks or less by virtue of the existence of the Panama Canal was as spectacular an achievement as the constant stream of cargo vessels and transports being moved through from one ocean to the other.

In recent years, however, there have been expressions of opinion that new technological developments have lessened the strategic significance of the Panama Canal to the United States.[15] It has been pointed out that America no longer relies upon naval power as her primary defense, and in any case she now has a two-ocean fleet, with enough fighting ships in the Atlantic and the Pacific to provide for any normal emergency to either without the necessity for reinforcement. Furthermore, a number of the newest U.S. aircraft carriers have a beam and canted decks too wide to pass through the Canal's locks. Transcontinental railroads and highways and jet aircraft will doubtless not entirely supplant the trans-isthmian sea route for the transport of bulk cargo, but they are means for swift wartime mobilization of men

9

and resources. Transcontinental pipelines now transport oil as cheaply as tankers do. Finally, because the Panama Canal is not a sea-level canal but a lock canal, it is critically vulnerable in a nuclear war. A sea-level canal would be as effectively blocked by an atomic blast, but repair and restoration of the sea-level canal could be done much faster.[16] Construction of a sea-level canal to supplement the Panama Canal through some region of Central America, Colombia, or Mexico appears to be a certainty for the future;[17] that fact alone cannot but alter the strategic significance of the Panama Canal to the United States.

A more important inter-oceanic waterway in terms of volume of international shipping may be the Suez Canal, through which transit 51 ships a day or more[18] of an average net tonnage size of well over 11,000 tons[19] bearing one-sixth of the world's ocean-going commerce.[20] But the Panama Canal, through which more than 30 ships daily[21] of a net tonnage size averaging 5,864 tons[22] carry about one-twentieth of the worl's sea-borne commerce, is of enormous significance to United States commerce. United States flag vessels are the largest users of the Panama Canal, accounting for about one-sixth of the total net tonnage during the fiscal year ending June 30, 1962 and for the largest number of transits.[23] The nine flags making the next greatest use of the Canal were Norway, Great Britain, Germany, Liberia, Japan, Greece, The Netherlands, Panama, and Sweden.[24] Of the eight principal trade routes which account for more than 75 per cent of the traffic through the Panama Canal,[25] five terminate in United States ports while a sixth is made up of American intercoastal trade; altogether, over 62 per cent of the cargo transported through the Canal begins or ends in United States ports. [26]

Other countries too besides the United States have a user's stake in the Panama Canal—those nations whose ships also carry goods through the waterway, and those which rely on the Canal for the transport of their imports or exports.[27] The dependence of users on a particular waterway is seldom absolute, for alternative means or routes of transportation may exist, and circumstances may render use of the alternatives economically feasible. In the case of the Panama Canal, construction of a broader, deeper sea-level canal in the isthmus region would markedly diminish or even end the commercial use presently being made of the Panama waterway.

10

But the Republic of Panama has a unique economic stake in the Panama Canal which would be crucially affected by construction of a supplementary sea-level canal through some other country.[28] By virtue of the controversial Treaty of 1903 to be discussed hereinafter, Panama is neither territorial sovereign of the Canal Zone nor operator of the Canal which has been cut through her territory. Yet the Canal brings economic benefits to Panama in a proportion greater than that to any other nation. Those benefits stem principally from four main sources: The centering of a vast trade brought by the thousands of ships which transit the Canal every year; the employment of thousands of Panamanian citizens by the Canal organization and other United States government agencies in the Canal Zone; direct purchases of supplies and services in the Republic by the Panama Canal Company and the U.S. armed forces; and from purchases made in Panama by Canal Zone residents, or contractors engaged in government work. Detailed figures compiled by U.S. Army sources soon after the January 1964 riots[29] are said to show that in 1962 the Republic of Panama received an estimated total of $84,395,000 in purchases and payments from Canal Zone sources, an amount about $17 million greater than the Panamanian national budget. Tourists that year brought in an additional $14 million in revenues. The United States is the largest employer in Panama: About 16,000 non-United States citizens, chiefly Panamanians, work in the Canal Zone for the Canal Zone Government, the Panama Canal Company and the U.S. Army and other federal agencies.[30] In the fiscal year 1962 full-time jobs with the Canal Zone Government were fairly evenly divided between Panamanians and U.S. citizens,[31] but Panamanians composed 77 per cent of the full-time work force of the Panama Canal Company.[32]

B. *Formal Treaty Arrangements and Practical Accommodations**

The Panama Canal flows through the territory of the Republic of Panama but is operated by the United States of America. A strip of land ten miles in width has been furnished the United States for the exploitation of the waterway. The rights of the United States derive from two important provisions of the Hay—Bunau-Varilla Treaty of 1903,[33] signed in haste only a few days after Panama had achieved its independence. The first of these is

11

that portion or article II of the Treaty which provides: "The Republic of Panama grants to the United States in perpetuity the use, occupation and control of a zone of land and land under water for the construction, maintenance, operation, sanitation and protection of said Canal [referred to in the preamble of the Treaty] of the width of ten miles. . . ." The second is article III of the Treaty: "The Republic of Panama grants to the United States all the rights, power and authority within the zone mentioned and described in Article II of this agreement and within the limits of all auxiliary lands and waters mentioned and described in said Article II which the United States would possess and exercise if it were the sovereign of the territory within which said lands and waters are located to the entire exclusion of the exercise by the Rpublic of Panama of any such sovereign rights, power or authority." The effect of article III is to make a distinction between what was conceded to be the "titular sovereignty" of Panama and the power of the United States to exercise those rights which it would have "if it were the sovereign of the territory." The Treaty was drafted by Bunau-Varilla, the Minister of Panama to the United States, in the course of one day,[34] but it would be naive to suppose that the formula employed was a hasty improvisation.

The establishment of a status for territory in which one state would retain sovereignty but another nation would exercise sovereign rights over the area was not without precedent. The leases of naval bases by China to foreign powers only five years before the Hay—Bunau-Varilla Treaty had made exactly such arrangements. In the Convention respecting the Lease of Kiaochow, for example, it was stipulated that "in order to avoid the possibility of conflicts, the Imperial Chinese Government will abstain from exercising rights of sovereignty in the ceded territory during the term of the lease, and leaves the exercise of the same to Germany. . . ."[35] Similar provisions are to be found in the leases to France and to Russia.[36] It may not be irrelevant to observe with respect to the juridical status of the Panama Canal Zone that the view of many learned writers on international law during this general period was that these leases constituted disguised cessions[37] or, at least, in light of the fact that the leases were for stipulated terms of years, cessions for a limited period of time.[38]

John Hay in 1904 first used the term "titular sovereignty" to describe the rights of Panama in the Canal Zone remaining after the grant to the United States provided for in article III of the Treaty of 1903.[39] Since that time it has become a patriotic sentiment among Panamanians that the United States visibly acknowledge Panama's residual sovereignty over the Zone. Considerable satisfaction was given to the Republic of Panama by the statement of the Treaty of 1936 with the United States that the Canal Zone constituted "territory of the Republic of Panama under the jurisdiction of the United States of America."[40] In more recent years there has been nationalistic insistence in Panama that the Panamanian flag be flown in the Zone where only the United States flag had flown since 1903. At length in 1960 further American recognition of the "titular sovereignty residing in the Republic of Panama with respect to the Canal Zone" was given symbolic form in the undertaking of the United States to fly the Panamanian flag together with the United States flag at one point in the Zone.[41] In 1962, in implementation of talks between President Kennedy and President Chiari on President Chiari's visit to Washington in June 1962, arrangements were made to have both flags flown together at various sites in the Canal Zone; by 1963 there was agreement between the two countries that the flag of Panama should fly wherever the flag of the United States was flown in the Canal Zone by civilian authorities.[42]

However, the basis upon which Panama has challenged the exercise of various rights in the Canal Zone by the United States has not been the language of article III, which indicates that the United States enjoys the full range of governmental powers within the Zone, but article II, which grants "the use, occupation and control of a zone of land and land under water for the construction, maintenance, operation, sanitation and protection of said Canal." In these words, according to the consistent Panamanian position over the last half century, are to be found the limits of the authority of the United States in the Zone.[43] Each exercise of jurisdiction by the United States must be measured against this standard and, if not necessary to the construction, maintenance, operation, sanitation, or protection of the Canal, is an infringement of the sovereign rights of Panama. At the time of the Suez crisis of 1956-57, the Panamanian Academy of International Law

13

declared that the cases of Suez and Panama were analogous in that both canals were constructed in territory not belonging to the entity which constructed them and that the Hay—Bunau-Varilla Treaty, which is the foundation of the rights of the United States, is "a contract of concession for international public service."[44]

Panamanian objections to the exercise by the United States of the "rights, power and authority" it would have "if it were the sovereign of the territory" were heard within a few months after the exchange of ratifications of the Hay—Bunau-Varilla Treaty in 1904. The first occasion for these protests was the extension of United States customs laws to the territory of the Canal Zone and the creation of ports of entry within the Canal Zone.[45] In this instance, the differences between the two governments were resolved by the so-called Taft Agreement of 1904. Although temporarily calmed, the fears of the Republic of Panama concerning the existence of a commercial enterprise established in its territory and in competition with its economy remained a cause of dissension between the two governments. The question of the Sovereignty of Panama over the Canal Zone again became a live issue when negotiations were in progress from 1923 to 1926 for a new treaty to replace the Taft Agreement. Both nations, before and after the abrogation of the Taft Agreement in 1924, expressed a willingness to treat and to compromise on many of the issues outstanding between them.[46] Each, however, started from a different assumption—the United States from the premise that it enjoyed full powers in the Canal Zone, from which any concessions to Panama would be in derogation, and Panama from the position that the United States had been accorded only limited rights in the Zone and had in fact been exceeding its powers under the Hay—Bunau-Varilla Treaty.

Although the attitude taken by the Republic of Panama toward many of the activities of the United States in the Canal Zone may be justifiable in political or economic terms—questions with which it is not proposed to deal here—its legal case lacks substance. If the language of article II of the Hay—Bunau-Varilla Treaty might seem to suggest the grant of a canal zone for limited purposes, any possible limitations on the authority of the United States are removed by article III, with its sweeping grant of "all

14

the rights, power and authority" which the United States would have if it were the sovereign of the territory "to the entire exclusion of the exercise by the Republic of Panama of any such sovereign rights, power or authority." The Panamanian position is, moreover, inconsistent with the contemporary understanding of grants of the same general character made during the same period. In suggesting that some of the treaties which separated technical sovereignty from the exercise of sovereign rights were actually concealed cessions, some of the authorities who wrote at the turn of the century went far beyond any position ever taken by the United States. The specific exemptions from the law of Panama accorded in various articles of the Treaty, such as the immunity from taxation of the property, officials, and employees of the United States provided by article X, are explainable as protection for these things and persons while they are within the territory of the Republic of Panama, as a defense against a possible extraterritorial application of Panamanian fiscal laws, or simply as restrictions on Panamanian jurisdiction inserted *ex abundantia cautelae*. The express enumeration of the rights enjoyed by Panama within the Canal Zone cannot be reconciled with the theory held by that country. It may be observed, however, that the language of article II, that the grant is "for the construction, maintenance, operation, sanitation and protection" of the Canal, upon which such heavy reliance is placed by Panama, does place one important restraint upon the plenitude of powers otherwise enjoyed by the United States. That qualification is temporal. If the zone should cease to be used for the support of the Canal, the rights of the United States in the zone would come to an end. But that is the extent of the limitation imposed.

To look simply to the theoretical extent of the powers of the United States within the Canal Zone under articles II and III of the Hay—Bunau-Varilla Treaty would give an altogether misleading impression of the actual relations of the Republic of Panama and the United States. A complex network of rights and duties of consensual origin controls the exercise of sovereign powers by the two countries. The exercise by the United States of those powers which it would have were it sovereign within the Zone is limited by restraints imposed by treaty, while at the same time the United States has been granted the right to carry on certain of its activities within territory subject to the jurisdiction of the Republic of Panama.

A number of the powers which the United States has in the past exercised outside the Zone and of those which it continues to enjoy today find their justification in being necessary to the operation and the defense of the waterway. Most intimately related to the management of the Canal is the right accorded by article IV of the Treaty of 1903 to use the rivers, lakes, and other bodies of water in Panama for navigation and for the supply of water, without which the operation of the locks would become impossible. Within the cities of Panamá and Colon, the adjacent harbors, and territory adjacent to the cities, the United States at one time had the right to acquire needed property by the exercise of the right of eminent domain.[47] In the Treaty of 1936 it was agreed that the United States would surrender its power of eminent domain and that the acquisition of needed lands outside the Zone would be the subject of agreement between the two governments.[48]

In addition to the lands which the United States has at one time or another utilized, the proprietor of the Canal has exercised certain rights of jurisdiction, now largely of historical interest, outside the Zone. From 1903 until 1936, the United States enjoyed a conventional right to intervene for the maintenance of order in Colón and Panama, the two terminal cities of the Canal, both of which lay within Panamanian territory. [49] Until 1955, the control of sanitation within these two cities likewise rested with the United States.[50] Still surviving is the right of the United States to operate the Panama Railroad across the Isthmus,[51] a doubtful advantage since the Railroad is being operated at a loss and is of questionable strategic value.

The United States is not alone in enjoying the use of lands and the exercise of rights outside the territory subject to its plenary jurisdiction. Panama has been granted a corridor through the Zone to connect the city of Colon with the rest of its territory.[52] Portions of the Boyd-Roosevelt Highway which intersect the Canal Zone have been placed within narrow corridors subject to Panamanian jurisdiction in order to avoid having vehicles enter the territory of the Canal Zone for limited distances, only to return to Panamanian territory.[53] Within the Zone, the United

16

States has accepted certain limitations on its powers with respect, for example, to the sale of goods to transiting vessels and sales from commissaries to nationals of the Republic of Panama[54] and to the categories of persons who may live in the Canal Zone.[55]

Others of the arrangements between Panama and the United States are solely a consequence of the fact that the two states are living in close propinquity and that persons subject to their jurisdiction move freely from the territory of one to that of the other. These understandings have their counterparts in similar agreements relating to the administration of boundary areas in other quarters of the world. The United States facilitates the administration of Panamanian customs and immigration controls on goods and persons entering Panama by way of the Zone through the provision of sites for customs houses and by affording immigration officers access to vessels arriving at the piers of Balboa and Cristóbal.[56] An extraordinary treaty[57] between the two governments implements the undertaking of article XVI of the Treaty of 1903[58] to provide for the detention and delivery by the one state of persons charged with crimes in the other. American military police and shore patrols are permitted to maintain order among the members of the United States Armed Forces who are within the territory subject to the jurisdiction of the Republic of Panama.[59] Panamanian nautical inspectors have been authorized by the United States to board and inspect vessels of Panamanian registry within the Canal Zone for the purpose of ascertaining whether there has been compliance with the laws of that country concerning maritime and labor matters.[60]

During the half century or more that the United States has exercised jurisdiction over the Canal Zone, the powers of the two countries with respect to the Canal Zone have increasingly been governed by detailed treaty arrangements rather than dictated by abstract considerations of sovereignty or of sovereign rights over this or that area. The jurisdictional competences of the two governments are not separated by the geographical boundary forming the periphery of the Canal Zone. Nevertheless, the basic instrument, the Hay—Bunau-Varilla Treaty of 1903, as modified, constitutes a starting point of legal right for any negotiations for further concessions upon the part of the one country or the other. Once a matter such as the authority of persons to purchase at

17

commissaries makes the transition from the unfettered control of the United States to a right regulated by treaty, the question becomes one which for the rest of time must be governed by agreement between the two countries.

In summation, the Panama Canal is operated by the government of a nation which has been granted full powers of jurisdiction within the Canal Zone—that area which has been provided by Panama as the territorial base from which the waterway might be constructed, managed and defended. The rights of the United States stem from the broad terms of the irrevocable grant made by the treaty concluded with Panama in 1903. In terms of political jurisdiction over the territory of the Canal Zone and of the provision of free transit through the Canal, the United States has retained, with only insubstantial diminution, the autonomy granted it by that treaty, an autonomy limited by the treaties and customary law governing the Canal. The control of the Canal and of the area through which it flows has been left by the U.S. Congress very largely to the discretion of the President, who exercises his authority through the Secretary of the Army and the Panama Canal Company. Both tradition and the strategic necessities of the waterway have dictated that there should be a strong military flavor to the administration of the Canal and of the Zone. In the present day, however, the plenitude of sovereign powers theoretically enjoyed by the United States under the "as if" formula of the Treaty of 1903 has been qualified by a large number of arrangements with Panama with respect to economic and fiscal matters. Debates about "sovereignty"[61] over the Zone hold greater interest for the legal metaphysician than for the lawyer.

C. *Canal and Canal Zone Administration*

1. *The operating organization:*

The Canal Zone, being territory under the jurisdiction of the United States, and the Canal itself, an instrumentality for the promotion of the national defense and the facilitation of interstate and foreign commerce, are subject to control by the United States Congress.[62] But from the beginning laws enacted by the Congress dealing with the Panama Canal have vested wide

18

authority in the President as regards the administration of the Canal and of the government of the area. The Spooner Act of 1902[63] empowered the President to acquire the territory and rights necessary for the construction of a canal and, through the Isthmian Canal Commission, to proceed to the excavation, construction, and completion of such canal. The Panama Canal Act of 1912[64] authorized the President to "complete, govern, and operate the Panama Canal and govern the Canal Zone, or cause them to be completed, governed and operated, through a Governor of the Panama Canal and such other persons as he may deem competent to discharge the various duties." Until 1950 the administrative organization through which the President exercised his authority to operate the waterway and govern the Zone was called collectively The Panama Canal, and was a part of the executive branch of the Government of the United States. In addition certain business operations incident to the operation of the Canal and the civil government were conducted by the Panama Railroad Company, which had originally been incorporated in New York State and was wholly owned by the Government of the United States.[65]

The most recent legislation enacted by the Congress for the governance of the Canal Zone and the Canal has separated the functions of operating the Canal and its ancillary facilities from the civil government of the area.[66]

Now maintenance and operation of the Canal and conduct of those incidental business operations once carried on by the Panama Railroad Company are done by the Panama Canal Company, a public corporation of which the United States is the owner.[67] The Stockholder of the Panama Canal Company is the Secretary of the Army in his individual capacity as the personal representative of the President of the United States for such purpose, and the Company operates under the management of a board of directors appointed by the Stockholder.[68] Operation of the Canal itself is entrusted to a managerial staff headed by the President of the Panama Canal Company, by tradition a general officer of the Corps of Engineers of the United States Army.[69] In view of the close relation between the civil government of the Zone and the operation of the Canal, the President of the Panama Canal Company assumes that office by reason of his appointment as the

19

Governor of the Canal Zone.[70] Activities of the Panama Canal Company directly related to the operation of the waterway are concerned with the transiting of ships, maintenance and improvement of the Canal channel, and maintenance and operation of the locks. The business operation incident to maintenance of the Canal and incident to the civil government of the Zone which the Company also conducts include vessel repairs, harbor terminal operations, a railroad across the Isthmus, a steamship line operating between New Orleans and the Canal Zone, motor transportation facilities, storehouses, an electric power system, a telephone system, a water system, and the operation of retail stores, restaurants, and housing for employees.[71]

The Congress has granted to the President the authority to govern the Canal Zone through a Canal Zone Government, of which the Governor is the principal officer.[72] As in the case of the Panama Canal Company, the President has delegated his supervisory functions with respect to the government of the Zone to the Secretary of the Army. Within the Canal Zone, the Government furnishes normal governmental services. Since private land titles have been extinguished within the Zone, the entire area is in effect one great government reservation.[73] The contents of the annual report of the Governor resemble those of a report by the mayor of an American city—the incidence of disease, the activities of the police and the firefighting service, revenues, education,[74] hospitals—plus a more unusual section on the Zone postal service, customs, and immigration.[75]

Congress has enacted for the Zone a separate body of law which has been codified as the Canal Zone Code.[76] In addition to those general provisions of the Code governing the operation, maintenance, and government of the Zone, the Code comprehends civil laws, rules of civil procedure and evidence, a code of criminal law, and those other laws having application to the Canal Zone. The law which has been enacted exclusively for the Canal Zone excludes the operation of corresponding provisions of the general law of the United States, such as the Criminal Code embodied in title 18 of the United States Code.[77] In some instances, special legislation adopted for the Zone makes applicable to that area the existing law of the United States,[78] or a statute indicates that the territorial application of the act includes the Zone.[79] Other laws dealing with various aspects of governmental activity are considered applicable in the Zone by reason of the fact that the Canal Zone Government is an arm of the United States Government.[80] But as to a great many other statutes, the situation is unclear, and it becomes a nice question of construction whether the act should be considered to carry any effect in the Zone.[81] The President, acting under both his implied powers and those specifically granted him by Congress, supplements the legislation applicable to the Zone and the Canal with regulations dealing with diverse matters ranging from the issuance of licenses for the sale of alcoholic beverages to the control of aliens.[82]

The courts which administer the laws applicable in the Canal Zone are the magistrates' courts of limited original jurisdiction[83] and the United States District Court for the District of the Canal Zone.[84] The United States District Court has jurisdiction over criminal and civil actions which exceed the jurisdiction of the magistrates' courts, appeals from the magistrates' courts, actions involving laws of the United States which apply to the Canal Zone, and any other matters concerning which jurisdiction has been conferred by the Canal Zone Code or other federal law.[85]

The Governor of the Canal Zone, who is as well the President of the Panama Canal Company, is the chief executive of a highly centralized administration. But in the critical area of conduct of relations with the Republic of Panama, authority is divided between the Governor and the Ambassador to Panama, each of whom speaks for the United States to authorities of the Government of Panama.[86] In the past, disagreements between Ambassador and Governor have created problems in relations with Panama.

With regard to the defense and protection of the Canal and Canal Zone there is also a division of authority between the Governor and the Army. In the event of war or if a war is imminent, the President of the United States is authorized by statute to vest full control of the Canal and Zone in an army officer.[87] At present, the delimitation of authority as between the Commander in Chief, Southern Command, who commands the troops stationed in the Canal Zone, and the Governor, himself an army officer, is governed by an executive order[88] which stipulates that in the event of a conflict of views between the two as to whether

21

a matter pertains to the military defense of the Zone, the views of the Commander in Chief, Southern Command, are to prevail. The Governor has a right of appeal to the President of the United States, who is the ultimate arbiter of the question.

2. *Canal Tolls*:

From the beginning the Panama Canal has had for the United States a dual purpose—commerce and defense. Viewed as a commercial enterprise, the Canal does, for example, shorten the water route between New York and San Francisco by 7,873 nautical miles, or the water route between New York and Yokohama by 5,705 nautical miles,[89] saving time and distance for United States and world shipping. Viewed as an instrument for the defense of the United States, the Canal permits the flexible deployment and logistic support of American naval and military forces, while the Canal Zone serves as a strategically located military base.

Understandably, perhaps, in the financial history of the Panama Canal there has been some lack of precision in determining what part of all the expenses related to construction, operation, and maintenance of the Canal ought to be recovered through tolls collected from commercial users of the waterway, and what part should be borne by the United States itself as a cost of national defense.

Since the opening of the Canal to commercial traffic in 1914, the toll rate actually paid by vessels carrying passengers or cargo has been 90 cents per net vessel-ton of 100 cubic feet of actual earning capacity.[90] In 1948 President Truman prescribed an increase in toll rates to the then statutory maximum of $1.00 per net vessel-ton, but at the request of Congress, prompted by the protests of the shipping industry, the rate increase was postponed and finally cancelled. Instead the President prepared a study of the organizational aspects of the Canal operation and submitted it to Congress together with his recommendations for change. Under the then-existing tolls policy, revenues from tolls, together with profits from the Canal's business operations, were supposed to produce an amount sufficient to recover: (1) A 3 per cent return on the capital investment of the United States Government in the Canal; (2) the costs of operating and maintaining the Canal; (3) the net cost of civil government in the Zone; and (4) the cost of transiting United States Government vessels. The study revealed that, unless the fiscal criteria governing Canal operations were revised, the toll rate would have to be increased to cover projected operating deficits.[91]

In consequence of the President's study, Congress, by Act of September 26, 1950[92] effected the major reorganization of Canal and Canal Zone administration heretofore discussed. Among provisions in the Act designed to allocate the costs of Canal operation more equitably between users of the waterway and the United States Government were: (1) The interest on the capital investment of the United States Government was changed from 3 per cent to the going rate for long-term Treasury Bonds; (2) interest accrued during the construction period of the Canal was to be disregarded for the purposes of computing interest on the capital investment; (3) free transit of United States Government vessels was eliminated for accounting purposes; and (4) the supporting business activities previously operated by the Panama Railroad Company were to bear a proportionate share of the cost of the Canal Zone Government from which they had hitherto been exempted.[93] The Act of September 26, 1950 contains the following tolls formula: "Tolls shall be prescribed at rates calculated to cover, as nearly as practicable, all costs of maintaining and operating the Panama Canal, together with the facilities and appurtenances related thereto, including interest and depreciation, and an appropriate share of the net costs of operation of the agency known as the Canal Zone Government."[94] This basis for the assessment of tolls, which was further particularized in other provisions of the Act of 1950, was designed to put the Canal upon a sounder financial footing, while, through various accounting devices, keeping tolls from rising to a level which would reflect the full cost of operating the Canal.[95]

No express provision of the statute requires that, in the fixing of tolls, account be taken of reimbursement to the Treasury of capital supplied by the United States for the construction of the Canal. Such repayment comes, if at all, only in the form of liquidating dividends paid to the Treasury by the Panama Canal Company out of its retained revenues.[96] These dividends are to be paid only after the Company has set aside from its net income sufficient funds to meet "its necessary working capital require-

23

ments, together with reasonable foreseeable requirements for authorized plant replacement and expansion." The provision of such reserves for expansion and improvement is not obligatory and is wholly contingent upon the availability of funds over and above those stipulated by statute as required for operation and maintenance, interest, and depreciation.

The financial history of the Panama Canal gives every indication that the United States Government will never be in the position of recouping its initial investment in the Canal through liquidating dividends while at the same time securing assets equivalent to that investment. A total of $48,994,010 has been paid to the United States as liquidating dividends;[97] the net direct investment, as to which interest must be paid, stood at $328,171,297 at the end of fiscal year 1962.[98]

Private users of the waterway have contended that despite the new tolls formula Panama Canal tolls continue to be overburdened with costs of United States national defense. In 1956 a number of shipping companies employing the Canal brought suit against the Panama Canal Company, charging that excessive tolls had been exacted from them from the time of the coming into force of the 1950 legislation.[99] As grounds for their suit the plaintiffs used the Comptroller General's criticism in 1955 of the Panama Canal Company's accounting procedures that the Act of 1950 did not authorize the Company to charge losses sustained by its supporting business activities against the income of the Canal.[100] The shipping companies argued that the supporting business activities were not exclusively engaged in serving the Canal, but served all U.S. Governmental activities in the Canal Zone, referring primarily to the Armed Forces, and also the Republic of Panama and the public generally, and ought not therefore to be included in the tolls base.[101] The Panama Canal Company in turn took the position that much of the losses sustained by its supporting business activities was the result of "fringe benefits" to the employees and users of the Canal and were therefore, under the terms of the Act of 1950, properly includible in the costs of operating the Canal.[102] The outcome of the litigation, which eventually made its way to the Supreme Court of the United States, was to deny any remedy to the plaintiffs. The Court said that the problem was one "in the penumbra

24

of the law where generally the Executive and the Legislative are supreme," so that "the controversy at present is not one appropriate for judicial action."[103] Congress appears to have acquiesced in these accounting procedures of the Panama Canal Company. In 1960 the House Committee on Merchant Marine and Fisheries adopted a report stating that there was no need for new legislation expressly authorizing those procedures inasmuch as "the present practice of the Panama Canal Company in allocating the major part of overhead of supporting services to the account of tolls is proper and is in full compliance with the law as it now reads."[104]

III. "CAUSES OF CONFLICT BETWEEN THE TWO COUNTRIES. . . ."

The special Ambassadors under the Agreement of April 3, 1964 whom the Republic of Panama and the United States have designated "to seek the prompt elimination of the causes of conflict between the two countries" cannot be in doubt about what those "causes of conflict" are. For years representatives of the two nations have been talking about: (1) The amount of money the United States ought to pay for occupation, use, and control of the Canal Zone; (2) equality of opportunity and treatment as between Panamanians and United States citizens with respect to employment in the Zone; (3) increased opportunities for participation by private Panamanian commerce and idustry in the Market offered by the Canal Zone; and (4) some alteration in Panama's present status of perpetual exclusion from the exercise of sovereign rights in the Zone.

A. *The Annuity to Panama*

As "the price or compensation for the rights, powers and privileges granted" by Panama to the United States in the Hay—Bunau-Varilla Treaty of 1903, the United States agreed to pay Panama $10,000,000 in gold coin and also to make an annual payment of $250,000 in gold coin.[105] The $250,000 annuity to Panama was changed to $430,000 by the Treaty of 1936,[106] but the change was more an adjustment in terms of currency value than a basic increase in amount: In 1934 the weight of the United States gold dollar had been reduced, and the annuity increase, retroactive to 1934, reflected the change in the gold content of the dollar.[107] By the Treaty of 1955 the annuity was increased to $1,930,000, the present rate.[108]

Panama claims that the annuity she has been receiving from the United States is not just and adequate compensation for use of Panama's "greatest natural resource"—her geographical position which has made possible the construction of an inter-oceanic canal which the United States operates as a commercial enterprise and uses also for a military base. At the time of the Suez crisis of 1956-57, the Panamanian Academy of International Law noted that the annuity paid to Panama in the years before 1956 amounted to no more than the yearly sum paid before 1903 to the territorial sovereign for the trans-isthmian railway concession alone. The Academy pointed out by contrast that at the time of the nationalization of the assets of the Suez Canal Company in Egypt, that Company was paying 7 per cent of its gross profits to the Egyptian Government under an agreement of March 7, 1949.[109]

B. *Unequal Treatment Respecting Jobs and Wages*

When the Panama Canal was being built skilled employees, most of whom were United States citizens, were paid in gold, while local laborers from Panama and the Caribbean were paid in silver.[110] The distinction between "gold" Canal employees and "silver" employees, which began as a classification of payment, evolved into a symbol of the most rigid discrimination: Until 1946, when the accepted signs "gold" and "silver" were unobtrusively painted over throughout the Zone, even separate facilities like rest rooms, drinking fountains, and post office windows were assigned to each class.[111] The grosser inequalities of the "gold-and-silver" days are gone now from the Zone. But Panama still complains that her nationals receive discriminatory treatment with respect to wages and employment opportunities in the Zone.

For years Canal Zone agencies had followed the practice of dividing Canal jobs into two categories—"U.S. rate" and "local rate." Non-United States citizens were, however, eligible for "U.S. rate" positions if qualified, and when put into such positions were paid at the same rate as United States citizens but without the overseas wage differential provided for the latter. The separation of positions into the two categories, while perhaps not discriminatory in fact, gave an appearance of discrimination which was resented by Panama.[112]

Diplomats of both countries hoped that there would be an end to the quarrel with the arrangements arrived at in the Treaty of 1955.[113] But legislative implementation of the understandings set out in that Treaty did not come until several years later. Since

February 22, 1959, the basic wage for any employment grade level in U.S. Government agencies in the Canal Zone is the same for United States and Panamanian citizens. Rates of pay are established regardless of citizenship on a U.S. wage-base for those positions which would normally be recruited from the United States and on a lower Canal Zone wage-base for occupational categories which can be filled by recruitment in Panama. However for employees who are United States citizens, regardless of the occupational category which they fill there are approved additives which include a tax factor and a 25 per cent tropical differential.[114]

The wage increment representing an overseas differential, and some other employment benefits which United States citizen employees alone enjoy, cause a certain amount of irritation among Panamanian employees holding comparable positions. But the larger complaint of Panama is that the United States has continued to keep United States citizens in the higher paying, more important occupational posts, and has restricted access of Panamanian nationals to skilled and supervisory positions.[115] In the period February 1959 to June 1962 the number of non-United States citizens in higher-paid U.S. wage-base positions increased 417 per cent, from 144 to 618.[116] It would seem, however, that that stepped-up program to utilize Panamanians for skilled staff positions has come very late.

C. *Panamanian Participation in the Canal Zone Market*

The primitive conditions which prevailed sixty years ago in the mangrove swamps of the Isthmus of Panama required the United States to undertake a remarkable agglomeration of commercial activities and services which in more highly developed areas would have been supplied by local private enterprise. For example, when Canal construction was in an early stage, the Company had to provide living quarters for its employees and officials, and so it entered the hotel business.[117] To furnish food and other necessities to Canal laborers at low prices the Company opened commissaries where it sold goods it had manufactured or processed itself, and merchandise it had imported duty-free.[118] Because at first local firms did not exist or could not be depended upon for the regular supply of ships' stores to transiting vessels, the United States itself undertook a lucrative supply trade to ships passing through the Canal.[119]

But as Panamanian commerce and industry developed, to local merchants there seemed to be less and less reason why the United States of America should continue to be in the business of hotel operation, cosmetics manufacture, or coffee roasting in the Canal Zone; or why that foreign sovereign should have a monopoly of the sale of luxuries to visiting tourist ships; or why Company commissaries should be permitted to sell untaxed, low-priced goods even to Panamanians—the merchants' own market.

The United States responded to these local commercial pressures over the years, and in the Treaties of 1936 and 1955 restored a number of economic advantages to private Panamanian enterprise. The privilege of buying at the Company's commissaries was restricted to employees of the Canal or the United States by the Treaty of 1936;[120] the Treaty of 1955 closed the commissaries to Panamanian employees who did not reside in the Zone.[121] In 1936 the United States gave up the sale of luxury goods to transiting vessels,[122] and in 1955 it agreed to refrain from selling any goods other than fuels and lubricants to ships passing through the Canal.[123] The spacious old Hotel Washington was among the properties of the United States conveyed to Panama free of cost by the Treaty of 1955.[124] In the Treaty of 1955 the United States also undertook, so far as was feasible: (1) To import merchandise for resale in commissaries or post exchanges only from the United States or from Panama, so as to eliminate unfair competition with Panamanian merchants required to pay import duties; (2) to afford Panamanian enterprises an opportunity to compete for the sale of supplies, materials, and equipment for use in the Zone; and (3) gradually to terminate the manufacturing and processing of goods when it is determined that such goods are available from Panamanian sources in sufficient quantities, at reasonable prices, and of satisfactory quality.[125]

The Panama Canal Company did go out of the coffee roasting business in 1961; now the Zone's blended coffee requirements are obtained from the United States. Furthermore, in 1962 the Company was contemplating the discontinuance of its dairy operations, "inasmuch as large surpluses of raw milk were said to be

29

available from approved Panamanian dairies on a continuing basis and at reasonable prices."[126] However implementation of these provisions of the Treaty of 1955 seems to progress slowly. As late as 1962 Presidents Kennedy and Chiari were announcing that the question of increased participation by Panamanian private enterprise in the market offered by the Canal Zone would be one of the first concerns of the representatives who were to discuss differences between their two countries.[127]

D. *U.S. Sovereignty in Perpetuity in the Zone*

The possibility that the present régime of the Canal Zone will continue on without change in perpetuity is undoubtedly the greatest irritant in Panamanian-American relations from Panama's point of view. To most Panamanians it seems intolerable that, by virtue of a treaty concluded sixty years ago with their infant country, there should exist forever in the middle of their territory a foreign sovereign's privileged enclave. They very much resent what they call the typically colonial attitudes of the "Zonians"—American employees of the Canal organization many of whom are members of families that have resided in the Zone for two or three generations. The Panamanian who can by crossing a street enter the Canal Zone will there come under the rule of a different language, different laws, and different courts; and he will encounter alien inhabitants who have never attempted any kind of assimilation to his customs, and who would even deny his country's titular sovereignty over their compound.

To assuage Panamanian nationalistic sentiments the United States has tried in a number of ways short of treaty revision to take the sting out of its exercise of sovereignty in the Zone—and its efforts have met with fervent Zonian opposition. Panamanian demonstrations on their Independence Day in November 1959 which ended in rioting led to the 1960 undertaking of the United States to fly both U.S. and Panamanian flags together at one point in the Zone.[128] Zonian defiance of the further undertaking in 1963[129] that the United States flag when flown in the Zone by civilian authorities would always be accompanied by the Panamanian flag resulted in the riots of January 1964. The U.S. decisions to use Panamanian postage stamps with a Canal Zone cancellation in the Zone postal system, and to recognize in the Zone

30

exequaturs issued by Panama to foreign consuls to the same extent that such exequaturs are recognized within the territory of Panama,[130] were challenged in a suit brought by a Canal Zone resident

In the forthcoming negotiations the United States will undoubtedly propose further such concessions touching the régime in the Canal Zone but not affecting U.S. operation and control of the Canal or Zone Government. At no time in the past months did it seem to be Panama's intention to insist on fundamental alteration in control of the Canal, and now it appears that she does not plan to press for formal treaty revision in the negotiations of the next several months.[132] But responsible Panamanians like Dr. Octavio Fábrega, the Foreign Minister who negotiated the Treaty of 1955 for Panama, have indicated that it is Panama's ultimate objective to eliminate the perpetuity clause from the treaties which bind the two countries.[133]

IV. FUTURE ARRANGEMENTS FOR THE PANAMA CANAL

The immediate question which United States representatives must face in negotiations with Panama is: To what extent can the United States accede to legitimate Panamanian demands for change in the Canal Zone régime while still retaining the control necessary to safeguard vital U.S. interests there? However in the past several years there has come to be discussed with increasing seriousness the possibility of such radical alteration in the régime of the Panama Canal as internationalization, regionalization under the O.A.S., or nationalization. The acceptability to the United States of any of these long-range solutions would seem to depend, among other things, upon a reassessment of the continuing military and strategic importance of the Canal and Canal Zone to the United States, and upon the probability of construction of a sea-level canal serving the same trade routes.

It was President Truman at the Potsdam Conference in 1945 who is said to have made an early suggestion that the Panama Canal, along with some other international watercourses, be made a free waterway for the passage of freight and passengers of all countries, under international regulation of its navigation.[134] In 1960 Senator Aiken, upon his return from a study mission which took him to Panama, proposed that one possible way out of the continuing conflict between the United States and Panama over the Panama Canal would be the "internationalization" of the Canal under the auspices of the United Nations or the O.A.S.[135] However it is very much to be doubted whether internationalization of the Panama Canal is or ever will become an official policy of the United States. Neither does internationalization appear to be a solution acceptable to Panama: In August 1956 the Panamanian Minister to Egypt upheld the action taken by Egypt in nationalizing the assets of the Suez Canal Company and stated that Panama would never allow the Panama Canal to be placed under international control.[136]

Nationalization of the Canal by Panama may indeed be that

country's long-range objective. There have been reports that the U.S. Department of State has also had under consideration a program that envisions shifting the management of the Canal and Zone from military to civilian control, inclusion of Panamanians in the board of directors of the Canal Company, and perhaps ultimate transfer of the Canal to Panama. That long-term program is said to have met with opposition from the Pentagon, however.[137]

Discussion of future arrangements for the Panama Canal must necessarily take account of the possibility of construction of a sea-level canal linking the Atlantic and Pacific Oceans. The sea-level canal proposal is also a long-range objective. On February 14, 1964 Secretary of State Rusk said, when questioned about the sea-level canal: "It may be decades before one is needed. It certainly will be at least a decade before one could be built, and that would require careful negotiation with a country or countries about engineering surveys and sites and costs and things of that sort."[138] However, the United States and Colombia have already begun a study of the feasibility of cutting a sea-level canal through that country.[139] Interest in such a canal has been heightened by publication of estimates by the Atomic Energy Commission that the cost of digging a sea-level canal would be substantially lessened if the excavation were done with nuclear explosives.[140] A study prepared by the Panama Canal Company had shown that, with conventional construction methods, the cheapest way to build a sea-level canal would be conversion of the present Canal at a cost of almost $2.3 billion dollars.[141] But in 1960 the Atomic Energy Commission prepared an analysis of the costs of construction for various proposed routes using nuclear explosives. The Commission's cost estimates have since been reduced, because of the development since 1960 of thermo-nuclear explosives using less costly fissionable materials. It now appears that a sea-level canal excavated with nuclear power can be built through Panama along the Sasardi-Morti route for $500 million or even less; through northern Colombia for about $780 million; through Nicaragua-Costa Rica for about $1.24 billion; or along the Tehuantepec route in southern Mexico for about $1.5 billion.[142]

May 5, 1964

33

PART TWO
THE FORUM

THE SIXTH HAMMARSKJÖLD FORUM

May 28, 1964

Participants

JOSEPH A. CALIFANO, JR.
Special Assistant to the Secretary and Deputy Secretary of Defense

JOSEPH SIMPSON FARLAND
United States Ambassador to the Republic of Panama, 1960-63

VICTOR C. FOLSOM
Vice President and General Counsel, United Fruit Company

RICHARD REEVE BAXTER
Professor of Law, Harvard Law School

THE FORUM: A SUMMARY OF THE PROCEEDINGS *

This sixth Hammasrkjöld Forum was a discussion of another very current problem, the Panama Canal. It was presented on May 28, 1964, only about eight weeks after the United States and Panama had resumed diplomatic relations, interrupted since the January riots, and had agreed to appoint special ambassadors to seek prompt elimination of causes of conflict between the two countries.

The first speaker was Professor Richard R. Baxter of the Harvard Law School.

THE FUTURE OF THE PANAMA CANAL
by
R. R. BAXTER

I propose in these remarks to confine myself to the Panama Canal and not to explore the broader question of relationships between the United States and Panama. The riots of January, 1964, were symptoms. The procedure in the Council of the O.A.S. (the Organization of American States) and in the Inter-American Peace Committee whereby the two countries were induced to resume relations and to negotiate their outstanding differences was preliminary medication. The disease—if this is not too strong a word— was the clash of interests between Panama and the United States over the Canal. There undoubtedly are other sources of infection but the diplomat, not the lawyer, is the specialist who must be called in on that aspect of the case.

President Johnson has said that from the outset of the dispute between the United States and Panama which broke out in January, 1964, the United States was prepared to do what was "fair, just, and right." No one can rightly dissent from the proposition that this is what we ought to do. But abstract principles do not

---

* Prepared by Miss Doris Carroll of the New York and Massachusetts Bars.

decide concrete cases in international relations any more than they do in the courts. Are there any rules or standards by which we can determine what is "fair, just, and right"? Or is the question rather one of striking a bargain with the Republic of Panama at arm's length? If there are rules or standards which we can apply, then it would seem that we need apply only these to the facts, just as we apply international or municipal law in deciding any other dispute. If a bargain is to be arrived at, the lawyer's role is not that of a law-giver but of a negotiator. This is not to say that these two approaches are entirely separate or distinct. It may be helpful, however, to see where we should station ourselves between these two extremes of doing justice and of bargaining.

The first thing to be considered must certainly be the stakes—the value of the Panama Canal to the United States. Strategic considerations come first. A powerful force for the construction of the Canal was, as Professor Padelford has told us, the awakening realization by the American people of "the influence of sea power and its peculiar relations, so far as the United States went, to an isthmian canal." I need not remind you of the importance that the Canal, once constructed, has had in two world Wars. Several years ago, in the heyday of the bomb, massive retaliation, and brinksmanship, it became popular to say that the Canal had lost its significance as a strategic passage for our two-ocean Navy. Large carriers could not pass through it, and one nuclear bomb would put the Canal out of action for the remainder of the war. But the first consideration argues for a wider canal or a new sea-level canal, while the second eventuality is contingent upon a nuclear war—an overriding condition on every aspect of human existence. A war has been fought over the other great waterway of Suez without the use of nuclear weapons, and an incidence of warfare, wider since than before the establishment of the United Nations, has not brought the use of nuclear weapons. Whatever might be the ultimate decision on the strategic import of the Canal, I think a contemporary naval view would be that Panama is certainly a *convenient* passage to have.

The Army's concern with the Canal Zone is less easy to put one's finger on. The passage is a defensive responsibility, but the Zone also serves as a military base of substantial importance for relationships with the armed forces of the other American Republics. A certain amount of training, such as instruction in special warfare and courses for personnel of the American Republics, is carried on there. It must be realized that the Zone is a military base as well as a naval passage.

In normal times, the strategic significance of the Canal is overshadowed by its commercial importance. About five per cent of the maritime commerce of the world passes through the Canal. Vessels under the United States flag are responsible for a plurality but not a majority of transits. A better indication of the extent of the dependence of this country on the Canal is furnished by the fact that well over half of the cargo, in terms of tonnage, passing through the Canal represents exports from or imports into the United States. Petroleum, coal and coke, scrap metal, lumber, and sugar are the five most important products passing through the Canal. These facts are impressive enough in themselves, but in these days of balance of payments deficits, an economical and efficient passage for exports contributes in a particularly powerful way to the health of our economy.

Against this background, what are Panama's grievances? Two words will sum them up—"sovereignty" and "money." Let us take up the easy one first.

The United States has within the Canal Zone "all the rights, power and authority . . . which the United States would possess and exercise if it were the sovereign of the territory . . . to the entire exclusion of the exercise by the Republic of Panama of any such sovereign rights, power or authority." Since the grant was made for the purpose of constructing and operating a Canal, the grant would terminate if the United States were ever to cease using the area for a canal, and of course we cannot convey the area to any third party. In terms of real property law, there is a possibility of reverter and a restraint on alienation. Panama has what has been called "titular sovereignty," and it is full recognition of this basic, underlying sovereignty about which Panama feels so strongly.

The Suez crisis of 1956 was naturally of great interest in Panama. In January of the next year, the Panamanian Institute of International Law adopted a declaration comparing Suez and Panama. It asserted that the territorial sovereign of the Panama Canal is the Republic of Panama and that the Hay——Bunau-Varilla

Treaty of 1903 is in essence nothing more than "a contract of concession for international public service."

How many flags will be flown and where they will be flown thus assumes a great importance in the eyes of Panamanians. If flags will make the people of Panama happy, the watchword would seem to be (borrowing from Evelyn Waugh) "Put Out More Flags." In retrospect, the United States seems to have been too stubborn about this question. It must be said in justice to our government that demands for recognition of Panamanian sovereignty have an economic dimension as well, because that recognition is in turn used as a major premise in reaching the conclusion that various rights of the United States in the Zone should be further confined. A legal controversy is, in part, being acted out symbolically.

If we remember the setting in which the Canal Zone was secured from the newly-founded Republic of Panama, it becomes somewhat easier to understand why some should see the very existence of the Zone as an anachronism. The formula of the 1903 treaty comes from the turn-of-the-century leases of territory for military bases. The ways in which we secure military rights abroad have undergone tremendous change since that time. Leased areas gave way to military bases which remained subject to the sovereignty of the grantor state; and in turn military bases have yielded to the provision of military facilities, often jointly used by the host state and the foreign state. The modern pattern disregards territorial boundary lines between mine and thine and instead allocates jurisdiction between the two states on a functional basis. If we were building the Panama Canal today, we would do it without a Canal Zone which looks suspiciously to Panamanians like a foreign colony set down on its territory.

We currently pay an annuity to the Republic of Panama of $1,930,000. If I may quote from the Declaration of the Panamanian Institute of International Law, "The Republic of Panama, . . . has never obtained from the United States of America a just or adequate compensation." What is a "fair rent"—if it is proper to use this figure of speech—is perplexing. We have no standard on which to go, since there is no going rate of annuity for inter-oceanic canals. What weight is to be given to the fact that Panama's economy benefits handsomely from the Canal, the Zone, and the users of the Canal? And surely it would be wrong to inflate the payments to Panama as part of a foreign aid program.

Other sources of friction, such as sales by the United States in the Zone, customs duties, and the employment and pay scales of Panamanian labor ultimately come down to demands for more money, not necessarily for the Government but for the economy of Panama.

Of one thing we can be confident—Panama will be a perennial Oliver Twist. Perhaps one way out would be offered by giving Panama a share in the gross revenues of the Canal or in the operating income, so that its financial take would vary with traffic through the Canal. In times of increasing traffic, this might have a calming effect, but one can foresee that if traffic were to decline, Panama would be heard to say that its revenues should not suffer on that account.

It would thus be comparatively easy to do the magnanimous thing in paying deference to Panama's sovereignty. But as to the money—for the Government of Panama, for Panamanian merchants, for Panamanian employees of the Canal—how far should magnanimity and fairness carry one?

If we were to look at the negotiating table, where this issue is to be fought out, the counters which we would see on the United States side are: (1) the legal basis in agreements with Panama for what the United States is now doing; (2) the fact that the United States is effectively in control of the Canal Zone; and (3) Panama's dependence on the United States in terms of trade, tourism, and the like. On Panama's side are the facts that (1) the Zone is set down in Panamanian territory; (2) the importance of the Canal to the security and trade of the United States means that this country really cannot brook interference with it; and (3) a small state has the capacity to create embarrassment to a large power.

But instead of considering the balance of advantage between the two nations in the negotiations, it might be more enlightening to consider, starting from scratch, what we actually need in order to keep the Canal going. What has happened to the Suez Canal is again instructive. The past half-century has seen four stages in the régime of the Canal: In the first it was operated by a foreign company within an Egypt under British protection. After the

41

Second World War, British control shrank from the protectorate to the Suez Canal Base, and then both base and company disappeared with the nationalization of the Canal. Today, like the Kiel Canal, the Suez Canal is administered by the United Arab Republic, fully sovereign within its own territory. Precisely who operates a canal does not seem to be of major importance if—and these are important "ifs"—it is efficiently run and if proper international agreements and institutions have been established to guarantee freedom of passage.

I must therefore bluntly put the question: Do we need a Canal Zone at all? The Zone is anachronistic in that we would not order our affairs in this way if the Hay—Bunau-Varilla Treaty were being negotiated today. It is abrasive to Panamanian susceptibilities. It is costly not only in terms of our relationship to Panama but also in dollars and cents. That cost might be justified when the Canal was being cut through the jungle, but the apparatus of a colonial administration really does not seem necessary today. I suspect that, despite reductions in staff and economies, there is a good deal of Parkinsonianism. How many people are actually required in order to run the Canal? How many Americans actually need to be brought down to Panama?

Thinking about the future of the Canal and the necessity of a Canal Zone brings us then to the possibility of a new canal, to be cut through Colombia, Nicaragua-Costa Rica, Panama, or Mexico. If the usable life of the existing Panama Canal is limited, perhaps a holding operation is called for, in which there might be a graceful yielding to some of Panama's demands, at the same time that the United States maintains its control over the Canal Zone. When a new canal is undertaken, it is inevitable that there should be a new treaty and a new régime, and I can say with considerable confidence that a Canal Zone, in the form we know in Panama, should not and will not be part of the new scheme.

There seems at present to be no indication of any Panamanian pressure for Panamanian administration of the Canal. Panama seems content to have the United States do the work of operating and defending the Canal and absorb any losses. There is not the same sentiment in favor of nationalization as prevailed in Egypt in the early 1950s, but the Suez Canal was and is a much more lucrative venture than the Panama Canal. Pressure there is for the

42

employment of more Panamanians and at higher rates of pay. In this respect there is a parallel between Panama and the Suez Canal before its nationalization. In the absence of any strong pressure to get the United States out, it is neither necessary nor helpful to talk in vague terms about the desirability of internationalization of the Canal. Internationalization seems to mean, in the minds of those who advocate it, administration through the United Nations or the Organization of American States.

The creative skills of the lawyer will undoubtedly be called for when it comes time to conclude an agreement for a new canal, in all likelihood a sea-level one. The problem of administration will lessen in seriousness, since a sea-level canal will be cheaper and simpler to operate and to maintain and will require far less technical services than the present Panama Canal. These factors in themselves will diminish the need for a separate and distinct Canal Zone cut out of foreign territory, whether that area be subject to the jurisdiction of the United States, the United Nations, or the O.A.S.

There are actually two sides to the problem of establishing a régime for a new international waterway. One is the technical aspect, which looks to what sort of operating agency should be established to run the waterway. This is essentially a managerial and technical task. It is one for which the U.N. and the O.A.S. have no more technical skill and expertise than anybody else—if anything, less. Since neither of them is in this sort of business now, it would be necessary for each to start from the ground up, with technical assistance being given to the U.N. or the O.A.S. instead of by it. If the major share of the money is to come from the United States, if the greatest use of the waterway is to be made by the United States, if the United States now possesses the skill and resources to construct and operate an inter-oceanic canal, is there any reason why friends and neighbors should be brought into the operation? Would they, indeed, have any strong desire to?

The other side of the régime for an inter-oceanic canal is of deeper international concern and of wider interest to the lawyer—the creation of institutions and rules for the maintenance of freedom of navigation. Each of the existing inter-oceanic canals has its basic law today—Panama the Hay Pauncefote and Hay—Bunau-Varilla treaties, Kiel the Treaty of Versailles, and Suez the Convention of

Constantinople of 1888, as reaffirmed in the Egyptian Declaration of April 24, 1957. The present-day administrator and guarantor of freedom of navigation through the Panama Canal is the United States. If, in any future régime, the participation of the United States in the operation of a new inter-oceanic canal were to be confined to the technical and operating side, it would be necessary that some other agency take over the responsibility to see that the canal would remain free and open to the ships of all nations. This is a role which might be filled by an international body, whether subordinate to the U.N. or the O.A.S. Although such an agency would have the ability to lay down rules and to determine whether they had been observed or violated, it would not have at its disposal armed forces to secure compliance with its rules and to guarantee the security of the canal.

The suggestion has been made that the areas traversed by the great inter-oceanic waterways, such as the Isthmus of Suez and the Isthmus of Panama might be ideal places for the stationing of U.N. forces, who would, while not employed elsewhere, protect the canals on which they would be based. This would be an attractive idea if two conditions could be fulfilled. One would, of course, be the establishment of standing U.N. forces, of which there seems to be no prospect at the moment, and the other would be the willingness of the United Arab Republic or of Panama or of any other state in which the canal might be built to have a United Nations base set down on its territory. And at this point, we would be back at one of the sore points in the history of Suez and Panama—the presence of foreign forces and a foreign base on the territory of the nation through whose land the canal runs. The two conditions which I mentioned seem to me to be so remote at the moment that we need not concern ourselves with this approach to the canal problem.

There are other problems of international administration. Would there be enough for a supervisory agency of the U.N. or the O.A.S. to do, if its mandate ran only to assuring freedom of navigation through a canal between the Atlantic and the Pacific, and not to the technical function of running the canal? A possible answer is that an agency to oversee freedom of navigation might have powers extending to Suez, Panama, and Kiel; this could be accomplished only with the consent of the United Arab Republic,

Panama (or the state through which the new canal might be carved), and Germany. Would there not be some fear that institutionalizing the concern of all members of the United Nations with the canal might lead to interference by nations now indifferent to the waterways? A non-hunter who is given a hunting license may turn into a devotee of blood sports.

"Internationalization" is far from being a panacea. A more modest objective therefore seems called for. As to a future canal, the answer may be a joint public corporation, control of which would take into account the interests of the territorial sovereign and the financial and technical contribution of the United States, as well as the interests of the users. Joint corporations of the kind I envisage have been employed with some success in European public enterprises of international concern. A new treaty, confirming and regulating freedom of navigation through the waterway, would also be called for, but for that the common law is already well established. Finally, the United States might continue to bear the responsibility of assuring the security of the waterway and guaranteeing freedom of navigation. These are modest goals, but no less worthy of consideration for that. If a new canal linking the waters of the Atlantic and Pacific Oceans is to be constructed sometime during the next quarter century, it is already high time to start thinking about the legal régime of the new watercourse. And if a new canal will have to be built and new institutions created for it, there is less reason for alarm about Panama and all the more reason for moderation in our approach. If we are wrong— to the extent that anyone can determine this in a context which is partially one of negotiation, bargain, and compromise—we should heed the words of President Wilson, spoken with reference to another dispute with another country over the Panama Canal:

> ". . . We are too big, too powerful, too self-respecting a nation to interpret with a too strained or defined reading the words of our own promises just because we have power enough to give us leave to read them as we please. The large thing to do is the only thing we can afford to do, a voluntary withdrawal from a position everywhere questioned and misunderstood. We ought to reverse our action without raising the question whether we were right or wrong, and so once more deserve our reputation for generosity and for the redemption of every obligation without quibble or hesitation."

DISCUSSION FOLLOWING THE ADDRESS

At the conclusion of Professor Baxter's remarks there were other comments on relations between the United States and Panama by Forum participants Joseph Simpson Farland, United States ambassador to Panama in the years 1960-1963; Joseph A. Califano, Jr., Special Assistant to the Secretary and Deputy Secretary of Defense, who was counsel for the United States at the 1964 hearings in Panama before the O.A.S. and the International Commission of Jurists; and Victor C. Folsom, Vice President and General Counsel of the United Fruit Company. A general discussion followed in which questions from the floor were addressed to the Forum participants. What follows is a summary of such comments and discussion.

I. HISTORICAL ROOTS OF THE CONTROVERSY ABOUT NATIONAL SOVEREIGNTY IN THE CANAL ZONE

Panamanian discontent about United States sovereignty in perpetuity in the Canal Zone has deep historical roots. Ambassador FARLAND began his talk by remarking that, to understand the problems extant in Panama today, we have to go back in history beyond 1903, the year of the signing of the Hay—Bunau-Varilla treaty which permits the United States to exercise sovereign rights in perpetuity in the Zone.

Ambassador FARLAND reviewed events leading to the negotiation in 1902-1903 of the Hay-Herrán treaty between the United States and Colombia for the construction of a canal through the province of Panama, then a part of the territory of Colombia; the unanimous refusal of the Colombian Senate on August 12, 1903 to ratify that treaty; the subsequent plotting for a revolutionary secession of the province of Panama from Colombia, aided in no small measure by the effects of M. Philippe Bunau-Varilla, former chief engineer for the original French Panama Canal firm and large stockholder in the New Panama Company, who had come to the United States from France for the purpose; the successful and almost bloodless revolution which took place in Panama on November 3, 1903, the U.S.S. *Nashville* having appeared in Colón harbor and stopped the transit of 400 Colombian troops sent to reinforce the garrison in Panama; United States recognition of the sovereign republic of Panama on November 6, 1903, three days after the revolution; and on November 18, 1903, the signing of a new Panama Canal treaty by United States Secretary of State Hay and M. Bunau-Varilla, who had been appointed minister plenipotentiary by the infant republic of Panama.

Ambassador FARLAND then contrasted the Hay-Herrán treaty, which Colombia had rejected on the grounds that it provided for too small an initial payment and too great an invasion of Colombian sovereignty in the territory, with the Hay—Bunau-Varilla treaty, concluded without the participation of any Panamanian national. "Hay had offered Bunau-Varilla a carbon copy of the treaty offered to and turned down by Colombia," said Ambassador FARLAND, "yet Bunau-Varilla for reasons of his own rewrote that treaty extensively, to the advantage of the United States." The Ambassador then pointed out four important differences between the Hay-Herrán treaty and the Hay—Bunau-Varilla pact:

The Hay-Herrán treaty empowered the United States to construct a canal through a zone ten kilometers wide, but the width of the zone was increased to ten miles in the Bunau-Varilla treaty;

The rights and privileges granted to the United States in the Hay-Herrán treaty were for a term of 100 years, with options of renewal, while in the Bunau-Varilla agreement the rights are granted in perpetuity;

The Hay-Herrán treaty expressly provided that the rights and privileges granted to the United States were not to affect the sovereignty of Colombia over the territory in which they were to be exercised, in contrast to the virtual cession of Panamanian sovereignty contained in the Bunau-Varilla treaty; and

The Hay-Herrán treaty had provided for three kinds of law courts in the zone—Colombian, United States, and mixed—but in the Bunau-Varilla treaty there is no such provision because United States authority was to be absolute in the zone.

"Here, then, is the crux of the differences between the United States and Panama today," said Ambassador FARLAND. "This issue of sovereignty in perpetuity is one that is engrained in the heart of every Panamanian, be he one year old or one hundred."

Mr. FOLSOM, drawing upon history he had been taught at school in Colombia, where he had received much of his early education, added further historical details antedating the treaty grant of sovereign rights in the Canal Zone to the United States which, he commented, "indicate that our conscience should have been bothering us a long time before it did."

As early as 1835, Mr. FOLSOM noted, there had been attempts by Colombia to arrange for the construction of a canal across the Isthmus, but it was generally assumed that the canal would be built and managed by private enterprise. Contracts had been entered into by Colombia in 1835, 1836, 1838, 1851, and 1855, but

48

every one was with private individuals or private companies, and not one of them mentioned or contemplated any grant of sovereignty to the concessionaire. Further, Mr. FOLSOM pointed out, the 1846 treaty of friendship and commerce between the United States and Colombia, then called New Granada, contained a solemn guaranty of the sovereignty of New Granada over the territory of the Isthmus of Panama through which a canal might be cut.

Mr. FOLSOM also noted that Colombians and Panamanians often talk about what they call a constitutional infirmity affecting the Bunau-Varilla treaty grant of sovereign rights to the United States: Panama did not adopt a constitution of its own until 1904; in the interim it must have been governed by the constitution of Colombia, which fixed the national boundaries and made no provision for altering them except by the regular process of amendment—such amendment certainly not to be effected by any treaty cession of national territory to a foreign sovereign.

As for the "perpetuity" feature in the grant of sovereign rights to the United States, Mr. FOLSOM noted what he termed the "legalistic" point that in the civil law there is no such thing as a contract "in perpetuity," although sixty years of ratification of such an agreement might overcome any original inherent weakness. "The point I am making is that, basically, our original contract 'in perpetuity' may have reached too far and may well have been unconstitutional under the constitution of Panama at the time the treaty was made; whether these initial infirmities have been cured by sixty years of observance of rights and obligations under the treaty is a fine point."

II. THE JANUARY 1964 RIOTS IN PANAMA

Mr. CALIFANO, as counsel for the United States at the 1964 hearings in Panama before the O.A.S. and the International Commission of Jurists, had gathered facts regarding the events in Panama in January. These had been gathered with difficulty at first in the explosive atmosphere of international crisis, but assembled in strength by the time of the extended hearing before the International Commission of Jurists. He presented some of the facts that had thus been gathered:

"I would like to give these facts to you tonight for two reasons. I think, first of all, that they give a perspective to what we are now embarking upon in our negotiations with Panama. The story of what happened during the riots does place a focus on how intense the nationalistic feeling of Panamanians is, how easy it is to touch off, and how the legitimate nationalism of the vast majority of the Panamanian people can be used by some sinister elements in their own country. We may have some very, very difficult times ahead of us in the coming negotiations. Secondly, the facts show what a tremendous advantage there will be to having a sea-level canal instead of a lock canal in the region: We would no longer need to have large numbers of civilians and military there to operate and to secure it. The 1964 riots show how explosive a situation can develop when so many, visible, American, civilian middle-class people have to be located immediately next to what is essentially a very poor country for the vast majority of its people —and most of the people of Panama live near the Canal Zone.

"I don't know how many of you have been to Panama. It is a country that is about the size of the state of Georgia. The Canal Zone, ten miles wide and fifty miles long, sits about in the center of the republic of Panama, and the Canal itself is in the center of the Zone. No fence, other than a fence protecting the back yards of some houses, separates the republic of Panama from the Canal Zone. Here in New York, for example, the Canal Zone would begin at the east side of Fifth Avenue, and the west side of the street would be in Panama. We have about 35,000 Americans living there, including our dependents; about 12,000 of these people are associated with the Canal Zone Government and the Company, and about 23,000 with the U.S. military.

"The emotional issue between Panama and the United States—that of 'sovereignty in perpetuity' in the Canal Zone— is made visible before the mass of the people by the controversy about flag-flying in the Zone: The Panamanians have increasingly pressed for assurance that both national flags would fly there. When President Kennedy and President Chiari met in Washington in 1962, they agreed that both flags would be flown at "appropriate" places. Ambassador Farland and Governor Fleming decided in implementation of that agreement that the Panamanian flag would be flown wherever the American flag was flown by 'civilian authorities'—language intended to exclude private homes and U.S. military installations.

"By the fall of 1963 we were ready to fly both flags together at seventeen locations, carefully selected because we realized that this was a very serious and emotional issue. We excluded all schools because we thought that we would have a particularly difficult problem there. We decided that the way to satisfy our obligation to the Panamanians was to fly no flag at all at schools. And this we did. We took down the American flag at Balboa High School during the Christmas vacation in 1963, and when the United States students returned there was no flag flying.

"The students at Balboa High School went to school for one day without the flag and then, on the morning of the seventh of January, they themselves raised the United States flag on the High School flagpole. Our authorities in the Zone immediately took the flag down. The students returned from their first class, and they raised it again. They then surrounded the flagpole, and many of their parents supported them.

"The Governor was, at this point, in this position: In the presence of the photographers who had gathered there he could have American policemen forcibly remove the students from around the flagpole in order to take down the American flag; or he could try to work the problem out with the students and their parents. He chose the latter course, and despite the events that occurred later, I don't think there is anyone in Washington who would fault him for that decision. I certainly wouldn't.

"The Governor began immediately to work with the students and parents to persuade them of the wisdom of having both flags or none fly at this High School. On the afternoon of January 8 the Governor decided to come to Washington because he thought he had the issue resolved, and, I might add, the Foreign Minister of Panama shared his feeling that this issue would be satisfactorily resolved, and so informed the Governor at luncheon that day.

"At four o'clock in the afternoon of January 8, at a Panamanian high school on the Fourth of July Avenue, which is just across the street from the Canal Zone and separates the Zone from Panama, a group of students in the liberal democratic party of the high school were having an installation ceremony. They had just won the election over the Castro Communist party in that high school. At four-thirty some of their members came in to report: 'There are Panamanian students marching into the Zone with banners and a flag, to plant the flag at Balboa High School.' These students of the liberal democratic party were, naturally, quite nationalistic, and they wanted credit for what was obviously a very significant and important act, not only in the student world in Panama but throughout the country. So they joined the march, and they effectively took *some* control over it.

"When the Panamanian students reached Balboa High School, which is a distance of about a mile into the Zone, American students who had heard they were coming had begun to gather. The Zone chief of police stopped the Panamanian students several hundred yards from the flagpole, said that he did not want any trouble, and talked to the leaders of the students for about fifteen minutes. The student leaders agreed that they would walk to the flagpole, hold their Panamanian flag out in front of them, sing their national anthem, and then return to Panama. But the leaders were unable to get their fellow students to agree to the plan.

"Finally, about an hour later, the leaders came back to the Zone chief of police and said: 'A delegation of five of us will do it.' Five students came up to the flagpole, protected by our police, carrying one inflammatory banner and their national flag. But when they reached the flagpole they said: 'We no longer want to hold out our flag; we wanted to raise it.' By now the crowd of

Americans present numbered about 500, and between 150 and 200 Panamanian students were in the area.

"The chief of police discussed the problem with the five Panamanians for about twenty minutes, and then it became clear that there would be disaster if they remained any longer. He requested them to leave. They refused to go. Then he shoved them away, back to the main body of Panamanian students.

"The moment the delegation of five reached the main body of Panamanian students, two things happened: First, some of the students began throwing rocks at the police, rocks which were not available to them unless they had carried them into the Zone from the route by which they entered. Second, the majority of the Panamanians bolted out of the Canal Zone, except for the students who were now carrying a torn flag. Those students were picked up by a Volkswagen bus and were driven out to Fourth of July Avenue, where they began parading their flag up and down the Avenue.

"It was now about six-thirty at night. The main body of students who had bolted out of the Zone, about 150 of them, scared a couple of people, broke some windows, and smashed at some cars on their way out. But when those students reached Fourth of July Avenue, cars were already burning there and a crowd of at least 1,000 people had already assembled.

"This crowd along Fourth of July Avenue increased with fantastic speed. By seven-thirty that night they numbered between 3,000 and 8,000. Panamanians armed with rocks and fairly sophisticated Molotov cocktails charged the Canal Zone police at three locations and penetrated the Zone in three places.

"We had only about 80 policemen on this Pacific side of the Canal Zone, and these policemen were unable to restrain the Panamanians. The police first fired tear gas, and then they fired their pistols, at first over the heads of the assaulting Panamanians and then into the ground in front of them. Finally at eight o'clock the Army took over at the request of the civilian authorities.

"When the Army took over, its first problem was to clear the Zone of Panamanians. The first act of our commander there was to send up a plane to broadcast, in Spanish and English: 'Everyone who has no business on the street, get back to your home in Panama or to your home in the Canal Zone.' He sent troops out

53

and forbade them from using their firearms without his specific permission. With one minor exception in which no one was hurt, only tear gas was needed to clear the Zone of Panamanians who didn't belong there.

"But there was a second problem: snipers. By ten o'clock that night sniper fire began to be received at the Tivoli Hotel, just inside the Zone border, and the snipers were wounding Americans. At first the general in charge dispatched a group of soldiers to the Tivoli Hotel, where the sniper fire was being received from a semi-circle of buildings in Panama facing the hotel, and told them to use shotguns loaded with birdshot which might discourage the Panamanian snipers without killing or wounding them. This action was unsuccessful.

"When the rate of sniper fire into the Canal Zone on the Pacific side increased to about 200 rounds an hour, the general sent a group of expert rifle marksmen to the Tivoli Hotel, and he gave them permission to fire their rifles only when he said they could. He said: 'When you fire, two marksmen must identify the sniper you fire at. You first fire to chip the cement or wood near him and scare him; and then you fire to wound him, and only as the last resort do you fire to kill him.'

"The rifle marksmen killed several Panamanians; we have no doubt about that. But the sniper fire, from that Thursday night through January 13, four days, reached over 500 rounds an hour at various times on the Pacific side of the Zone. During those four days we fired for only five or six hours; we would just clear the area and restrain ourselves.

"On the Atlantic side of the Zone we had much more serious property damage and much more severe sniper fire. Three American soldiers were killed by sniper fire, and twelve Americans were wounded. We received fire there for thirty-six hours before we returned a shot, and then we did so because the snipers were using women and children as hostages.

"During this time, when the special representative of the O.A.S. was in Panama and when Secretary Mann, Secretary Vance, and other officials had come from Washington, they constantly asked the Panamanian Government to do something to stop the rioting and sniper fire. Nothing happened. Nothing happened for four days. Finally, after four days, a force of about 2,000 Panamanian national guardsmen moved in and within three hours there was no sniper fire. They cleaned out the snipers on both sides of the Isthmus and, although the rioting had largely subsided, they cleaned out what few rioters there were.

"In the course of our investigation of the January riots in Panama we have learned that, although the first rioting may have been sparked by patriotic fervor, criminal and Communist elements in Panama took over the rioting for their own purposes. We have scores of photographs and motion pictures taken by Panamanians and Americans which show weapon stores and other stores being looted. Many of the wounds suffered by Panamanians were cuts in the arm from broken shop windows, incurred while looting.

"We know too that some leaders in the rioting were known and identifiable Communists—members of the P.D.P., which is the outlawed Communist Party of Panama, and people who belonged to the Vanguard of National Action, which is, openly and proudly, the Castro Communist party in Panama. We begged the Panamanian authorities to pick up ten of these ringleaders. They said they didn't have their names. So Secretary Vance furnished the ten names. But on the next morning six of these ten Panamanians were to be seen leading the march of the Panamanian people in honor of their 'martyrs' who were killed during the riots.

"Our lawyers and investigators, as a result of interviewing literally hundreds of people, discovered that on the first night Panamanians were frequently firing at their own people; many of the Panamanians that were killed were killed by bullets of a calibre the Americans didn't use. A gross example of the provocative behavior of sinister elements in Panama occurred at about nine o'clock on January 8, on Fourth of July Avenue: A Panamanian, walking along that street with a camera, pulled out a gun and fired two shots into the Panamanian crowd. One person fell from the shots. The Panamanian who had fired then put the gun under his arm, took a picture of the scene, and jumped into a taxicab and drove off.

"I do not in any way want to challenge what I think is legitimate nationalism on the part of the vast majority of the Panamanian population, but I think what I have just told you illustrates how easy it is for sinister forces to touch off that nationalism and use it.

"Finally, I should like to point out how the eventual construction of a sea-level canal would ameliorate the explosive situation of a large group of middle-class Americans necessarily located in what is essentially a very poor country. If we had a sea-level canal, we would not need the 12,000 Americans now employed in the Canal Zone Government and Company; assuming that we ran the sea-level canal, we would probably need only four or five hundred people. We would not need great numbers of military forces there to secure the sea-level canal, because such a canal would be virtually indestructible. We would need some military forces there for our larger commitments in the Western Hemisphere, but they would probably be stationed there under some sort of base-rights agreement."

During the question period Mr. CALIFANO was asked from the floor: "To what extent did the United States government explain to the Zone high school students and their parents, before January 7, the reasons for the decision not to fly any flag at the Zone schools?" Mr. CALIFANO answered: "The short answer is: 'obviously not enough.' One thing we have learned out of all this is that we need a much better system of communication with our own people living in the Canal Zone." Ambassador FARLAND added to that discussion:

"I think the people in the Canal Zone were woefully unprepared for what actually happened. When arrangements were being made in early 1963 to have both national flags flown together at various sites in the Zone, the Governor, the present Secretary of the Army, and I were highly concerned about the attitude of a small segment of Zonians—whether they properly understood what the Commission was doing, and the authority under which it was acting. When we adjourned I asked that a proclamation of some kind be issued from the White House indicating that we were acting in full accordance with the stated policy of the United States. That proclamation was not forthcoming. I would like to point out that on the first day of the January 1964 riots there was an article in the English-language newspaper 'The Panama American,' which has been anything but pro-U.S., clearly implying that there was only one area in the Zone where the Panamanian flag could legally fly, and that any arrangements for flying both flags or none at other places in the Zone were unauthorized."

56

III. PROBLEMS TO BE CONSIDERED IN THE COURSE OF FORTHCOMING NEGOTIATIONS BETWEEN THE UNITED STATES AND PANAMA

All of the Forum participants agreed that the probability of construction of a sea-level canal in the area would dominate U.S.-Panamanian negotiations looking to a new régime in the Canal Zone. Ambassador FARLAND noted that talks in Washington with Panamanian representatives in June 1962 were expressly premised on a contemplated sea-level canal. Said the Ambassador: "We informed the Panamanians that their request for renegotiation of the Bunau-Varilla treaty should be postponed during this interim because, in the event of a new canal being dug by nuclear or conventional means, the 1903 treaty would be moot and its renegotiation unnecessary; a new treaty would be necessary, and it would be on an entirely different basis than the one written by our friend the Frenchman. The Panamanians are agreable to this."

The contemplated construction of a sea-level canal in fact raises a host of new problems. For one thing, Ambassador FARLAND pointed out, there is the question whether we can use nuclear power to dig the canal without first effecting some change in the nuclear test ban treaty of 1963. "Incredibly," said the Ambassador, "when Bob Fleming and I were in 1963 appointed Commissioners to discuss with the Panamanians possible changes in the Canal Zone régime within the terms of the 1903 treaty, we were asking them for time during which a technical investigation dealing with the use of atomic energy for building the sea-level canal could be conducted. Yet at the same time other Department of State representatives engaged in negotiation of the nuclear test ban treaty were insisting that the limitation be put in that treaty which seems presently to forbid construction of a canal by nuclear means. While we were talking with the Panamanians, neither Bob Fleming nor I had any knowledge of the limitation contained in the test ban treaty."

Another new problem is: Shall the sea-level canal be built in

Panama or in Colombia? Ambassador FARLAND indicated that the decision could involve a difficult weighing of economic feasibility against diplomatic considerations. He said: "The Panamanians feel that there will be no leaving of Panama. I talked this over with Galileo Solis, the Foreign Minister of Panama, and I said that I, for one, do not care to trade old friends for new. But I also pointed out to him that we were faced with entirely new engineering circumstances which had to be considered in deciding where to locate a canal which will for economic reasons be built through use of nuclear energy."

And what shall be done in the meantime, until the sea-level canal is built, to improve the régime in the Canal Zone? Mr. FOLSOM, observing that he was a businessman as well as a lawyer, and that his firm, the United Fruit Company, is one of the biggest users of the Panama Canal, with a ship and a half in the Canal at all times had several suggestions for improvement. He thought that the Canal administration ought to be studied, and that some members of the Canal Company's board of directors ought to be Panamanians. "When I get the Canal Company report every year," he said, "I see there are lots of promotions, but I don't see many Panamanians in that long list." Mr. FOLSOM believed too that the Canal's accounting practices should probably be given a thorough overhauling. "The North Americans say we are just breaking even, but the Panamanians say we have got a lot of fancy bookkeeping going on."

Mr. FOLSOM was also of the opinion that the amount of the annuity the United States pays to Panama ought probably to be increased to meet Panama's needs. He would not, however, make up that increase in the annuity by any major raise in Canal tolls. He said: "I was a little shocked to read some place that Panama Canal tolls ought to be raised 30 percent and the whole 30 percent given to Panama. That certainly is an extreme position. It is obvious that any substantial increase in the tolls will not only be a hardship on Panama's own economy, but also on that of Chile, Peru, Ecuador, and all of the Central American countries which ship products to the United States through West Coast ports, not to mention the adverse effect upon our own economy."

A last comment from the floor was addressed to Ambassador FARLAND: "If there is no question but that a treaty with Panama drawn up today would recognize the rights of the traversed country to sovereignty and to partnership with the United States, why would it not be a dramatic reassertion of our renewed moral leadership in the world for President Johnson to say: 'Now we want to treat with you on the basis of the international mores of today, your retained sovereignty, and our partnership with you'?" The Ambassador replied: "I think we should take such a position. Ours is the greatest country in the world. We cannot be minimal in our approach, especially to a smaller nation. The Panamanians have been friends of ours for almost one hundred years and, despite everything, there is a wealth of good will there towards us."

CONCLUDING COMMENT

In concluding the Forum, the moderator, Mr. Tondel, quoted the following sentences from Professor Baxter's working paper:

"If the problem of the future of the Panama Canal is unique, the problem of Panama is not. How the demand for stability and the demand for change can be peaceably reconciled is a central problem of contemporary international relations and international law. If change is to come peacefully, the lawyer must become the architect of new institutions, a task which he cannot undertake to perform intelligently without an understanding of prior patterns and present needs."

Appendix

REPORT ON THE EVENTS IN PANAMA
JANUARY 9-12, 1964

*prepared by the Investigating Committee
appointed by
the International Commission of Jurists*

INTRODUCTORY NOTE

The International Commission of Jurists was requested by the National Bar Association of Panama to investigate a number of complaints of infringements of Articles 3, 5 and 20 of the Universal Declaration of Human Rights by the United States of America on the 9th, 10th, 11th and 12th of January 1964 in Panama.

The Commission appointed an Investigating Committee consisting of three well-known jurists to undertake the investigation:

Professor A. D. Belinfante of Amsterdam University (The Netherlands);

Judge Gustaf Petrén (Sweden);

Mr. Navroz Vakil, practising lawyer, Bombay (India).

The Commission now presents the unanimous findings and Report of the Investigating Committee. The methods and procedure adopted by the Investigating Committee are dealt with in the Report.

Quite apart from the importance of the issues involved in themselves, the Report marks one of the first occasions on which the provisions of Articles 3, 5, 13 (1) and 20 of the Universal Declaration of Human Rights have been invoked and construed authoritatively. While Article 13 (1) was not originally invoked, it is also considered in the Report.

In this connection it will be noted that the Investigating Committee relied in part on the provisions of Article 3 to construe both it and Article 5. In reaching its conclusions the Investigating Committee considered the relevant provisions of the European Convention on Human Rights and of the Inter-American Draft Convention on Human Rights. The construction placed by the Investigating Committee on Articles 3, 5 and 20 (1) of the Universal Declaration and the consideration given to the three great instruments referred to will be of considerable interest to jurists all over the world and should constitute a major contribution to the evolution of a practical jurisprudence in this field.

The Commission is indebted to the Governments of the Republic of Panama and of the United States of America, as well as to all those who assisted the Investigating Committee in its difficult work, for their assistance and cooperation. This cooperation provides a good example of a reasoned approach, based on legal rules, to a difficult international problem.

The Commission is under a debt of gratitude to the members of the Investigating Committee for their willingness to undertake this difficult mission and for the care and trouble which they took in the preparation of their Report. The Commission shares their hope that the work they have carried out will contribute to the growth of understanding, cooperation and amity between the two countries and their peoples; that the members of the Investigating Committee have contributed to this constructive objective will be their only reward.

The Report is presented as an impartial and objective assessment of the issues involved.

Seán MacBride
Secretary-General

REPORT ON THE EVENTS IN PANAMA
JANUARY 9-12, 1964

PART I

THE CONSTITUTION OF
THE INVESTIGATING COMMITTEE AND ITS WORK

1. On January 21, 1964, Dr. Jorge E. Illueca, President of the National Bar Association of Panama, in a letter addressed to Mr. Fernando Fournier, Member of the International Commission of Jurists, charged the military and police forces of the United States of America, stationed in the Panama Canal Zone, with violations of human rights on January 9, 10 and 11, 1964, in the cities of Panama and Colón. He requested the Commission to investigate the charges.

2. The letter charged the military and police forces of the United States of America with violations of Articles 3, 5 and 20 of the Universal Declaration of Human Rights of the United Nations. The allegations under the relevant Articles were:

Article 3: Everyone has the right to life, liberty and security of person.

The troops and police of the Government of the United States

61

of America stationed at the Zone of the Panama Canal, violated this right when opening fire on the defenseless Panamanian civil population, in both the cities of Panama and Colón, resulting in 15 deaths. In causing these deaths, the military and police forces of North America used .38 calibre, Smith & Wesson Special, and 7mm., 7.62 mm. projectiles.

Article 5: No one shall be subjected to torture or to cruel, inhuman or degrading treatment or punishment.

The North American military and police stationed in the Panama Canal Zone violated this right against the Panamanian civil population, in both the cities of Panama and Colón, by shooting at the Panamanian civil population. The North American troops used .38 calibre projectiles, Smith & Wesson Special, 7 mm., 7.62mm. 410 and bayonets.

Article 20(1): Everyone has the right of freedom of peaceful assembly and association.

On the 9th, 10th and 11th January, 1964, the Panamanian population made a peaceful use of this right in their own territory and the North American military and police fired small arms and teargas shells for the purpose of preventing the free use of such a right.

3. The Commission appointed a team of three observers to act as an Investigating Committee: Professor A. D. Belinfante, of The Netherlands; Judge Gustaf Petrén, of Sweden; and Mr. Navroz Vakil, of India. The Committee met on February 28, 1964, in Geneva and left for Panama on March 1, 1964. The Governments of the Republic of Panama and the United States of America gave their full assistance to the Investigating Committee.

4. The parties appearing before the Investigating Committee were represented as hereunder:

Republic of Panama:
DR. ELOY BENEDETTI
Legal Adviser to the Ministry of External Affairs

United States of America:
MR. JOSEPH A. CALIFANO
General Counsel to the Department of the Army
(Chief of the delegation and spokesman)

MR. STERLING J. COTTRELL
Deputy Assistant Secretary of State for Inter-American Affairs

Mr. John F. Wolf
United States Government Attorney

Mr. Dwight McKabney
Assistant General Counsel to the Panama Canal Company

Mr. Robert K. Donlan
Attorney to the Civil Division of the United States
Department of Justice

The National Bar Association of Panama:
Dr. Jorge E. Illueca
(Chief of the delegation and spokesman)

Dr. Eduardo Valdez

Dr. Diógenes A. Arosemena, G.

Lic. Rodrigo Arosemena

Lic. Carlos Bolívar Pedreschi

Lic. Guillermo Márquez Briceño

Lic. Ricardo A. Rodríguez

5. The Investigating Committee was graciously received by the President of the Republic of Panama, His Excellency Roberto F. Chiari, and the Foreign Minister of Panama, His Excellency Dr. Galileo Solis, as also by the Governor of the Canal Zone, Major-General Robert J. Fleming Jr., and by General Andrew P. O'Meara, Commander-in-Chief, United States Army Southern Command.

6. Immediately after its arrival, the Investigating Committee had several meetings with the representatives of both sides separately in order to secure agreement on the procedure to be followed. Although diplomatic relations between the Republic of Panama and the United States of America were severed at the time, the Committee insisted that in order to fulfil its task it was essential that both parties should be present at all the proceedings. The Investigating Committee adopted the following rules of procedure:

1. The official languages of the proceedings will be Spanish and English.

2. The Panamanian Bar Association will be requested to present a statement with each point of reference.

3. As soon as the Committee has received the statement of the Panama Bar Association, it will be submitted to the United States' representatives for a statement from their side.

63

4. The Committee will consider the two statements in order to ascertain the issues in dispute. This will be done at a meeting with both parties present.
At this meeting the evidence proposed on all disputed issues will be stated. For that reason the parties should be prepared to indicate the evidence available to them on these issues.

5. The hearing of such evidence that the Committee judges necessary and relevant will then take place. All evidence will be heard in the presence of both parties.

6. Each party should be represented at the meetings by *one* spokesman assisted by other persons, drawn from a list given to the Committee not exceeding six persons. The list of each party will be furnished to the other.

7. The terms of reference of the Investigation were agreed by the parties to include an enquiry into the following issues:

1. The death of fifteen persons during the events of January 9, 10 and 11, 1964, in Panama and Colón. Alleged violation of Article 3 of the Universal Declaration of Human Rights.

2. The shooting from the Canal Zone into the territory of Panama during January 9, 10 and 11, 1964. Alleged violation of Article 5 of the Universal Declaration of Human Rights.

3. The dissolution of a Panamanian students' assembly in the Canal Zone on the afternoon of January 9, 1964. Alleged violation of Article 20 of the Universal Declaration of Human Rights.

4. The alleged improper blockade of the Bridge in Panama and of the Corridor of Colón, during the events of January 9, 10 and 11, 1964.

8. The third issue above was later enlarged to cover the same field as that covered in the corresponding charge in the letter of January 21 quoted above. In addition to these four issues, it was agreed by the parties that written statements would be received covering allegations of inequality of treatment in the Canal Zone.

9. The Chairmanship at the hearings rotated between the members of the Investigating Committee.

Lic. Rodrigo Oreamuno of Costa Rica acted as Secretary and as Interpreter to the Committee; Mrs. Angela Fahlberg acted as Administrative Secretary.

The hearings lasted for approximately 100 hours, during the course of which 26 witnesses were examined by the Committee. The parties were also given the opportunity of questioning the witnesses. A larger number of documents was tendered in evidence; all documents presented by one side were communicated to the other. The Investigating Committee heard arguments by the representatives of both sides. The proceedings were tape-recorded.

The Investigating Committee, accompanied by the representatives of the parties, visited Colón on March 12 from 9 a.m. to 12 noon and a number of relevant places in Panama City as well as in the Canal Zone, on March 13 from 9 a.m. to 11 a.m.

The Mission left Panama on March 14, 1964.

PART II

INTRODUCTION

10. The history of the relations between the Republic of Panama and the United States is, in large measure, the history of the isthmus-canal of Panama. This history started even before the Republic of Panama came into existence, as soon as plans for the construction of a canal began to take form. It is not necessary to relate in detail the disaster of the French attempt to construct a canal, which ended in the abandonment of these plans at the end of the nineteenth century. The United States of America started where the French company left off, and concluded in 1903 a treaty with Colombia, in which this Republic granted to the United States the right to construct a canal and to acquire a zone of land on both sides thereof in the Colombian province of Panama. Panama, at the time, was part of the Republic of Colombia. This treaty, called the Hay-Herran Treaty of 1903, was not ratified by Colombia. Then, on November 3, 1903, the Colombian province of Panama proclaimed its independence. The young Republic of Panama, recognized by the United States of America on November 13, 1903, reached an agreement with the latter about the construction of a canal, the Hay—Bunau-Varilla Convention of November 18, 1903. This treaty is still in force and forms the base of the relations between Panama and the United States.

11. Article 2 of the treaty begins as follows: "The Republic of Panama grants to the United States in perpetuity the use, occupation and control of a zone of land and land under water for the construction, maintenance, operation, sanitation and protection of said Canal of the width of ten miles extending to the distance of five miles on each side of the center line of the route of the Canal to be constructed. . . ."

12. Article 3 that follows reads: "The Republic of Panama grants to the United States all the rights, power and authority within the zone mentioned and described in Article II of this agreement and within the limits of all auxiliary lands and waters mentioned and described in the said Article II which the United States would possess

65

and exercise if it were the sovereign of the territory within which said lands and waters are located to the entire exclusion of the exercise by the Republic of Panama of any such sovereign rights, power or authority."

13.   On the basis of this Convention a special territory on either side of the Canal, comprising about 650 square miles from the Atlantic to the Pacific, was created; it divided the territory of the Republic of Panama in two parts. The Canal was opened to traffic in 1914. The Canal has been of the utmost importance for the development of the economy of the Republic of Panama. It is in reality the mainspring of the economy of the Republic of Panama, as, apart from the direct revenues from the Canal, the presence of the Canal yields indirectly a substantial income from numerous other sources. On the other hand, the provisions of the Convention have given rise to controversy in regard to questions of sovereignty between the two Governments almost from the beginning (*i.e.*, from 1903) to the present day. It is not the purpose of this Report to propose solutions to the problems of interpretation of the 1903 Convention and the rights flowing from such interpretation. The Committee, however, considers it necessary to enunciate clearly the two interpretations placed by the parties on the clauses of the Convention quoted above.

14.   The Republic of Panama and the Panamanian Bar Association maintain that the interpretation of these clauses must be limited and governed by the overall purpose and requirement of the Convention, namely, the construction, maintenance, operation, sanitation and protection of the Canal. According to this Convention the sovereignty granted under the two clauses referred to above would be strictly limited to the aforesaid overall purpose and object. This interpretation was raised as early as 1904, when the Government of Panama claimed the right to control all ports, even in the Canal Zone, and purported to deny the right of the United States to establish custom houses and a postal service, on the ground that the latter were not connected with the construction etc. of the Canal. The United States, on the other hand, maintains that the Convention grants to the United States the exclusive control of and jurisdiction in the Canal Zone to the entire exclusion of the exercise therein by the Republic of Panama of any use, occupation, jurisdiction, rights, power or authority.

15.   The executive power in the Canal Zone is exercised by the Governor, who is appointed by the President of the United States. The Canal Zone government is under the supervision of the Secretary of the Army of the United States. The Governor is at the same time Director of the Panama Canal Company, a body corporate owned by the United States; the Company runs the Canal. The legislative power in the Canal Zone is exercised by the United States Congress

and the judicial power is exercised by a District Court forming part of the United States Federal Court System. The United States have established in the Canal Zone a settlement of American citizens employed in the Canal Zone administration or by the Canal Company, who with dependants amount to about 16,000 persons. In addition, there are residing in the Zone non-American citizens (chiefly Panamanians) also so employed. The entire civilian population, consisting of approximately 27,300 persons (1964), constitutes a separate community which is in no way subject to the jurisdiction or administration of the Republic of Panama. Furthermore, the military forces of the United States of America in the Zone with their families consist of about 20,000 persons augmenting the figure of the population of the Zone to about 47,000 in all.

16. The issue of the interpretation of the Convention of 1903 is, therefore, not an abstract problem but of great practical importance. Modifications in the 1903 treaty were made in 1936, 1942, 1947 and 1955. The main problem, however, remains unresolved; indeed it is this problem that gave rise to the subject matter of the current difficulties. The Panamanians desire recognition of the titular sovereignty of Panama in the Canal Zone; hence the raising of the Panamanian flag together with the United States flag in the Canal Zone has assumed considerable importance as a symbol of titular sovereignty.

17. The flag issue was one of the main causes of the violent disturbances in Panama of November 1959. On September 7, 1960, President Eisenhower took the "voluntary and unilateral decision" to fly the Panamanian flag together with the United States flag on Shaler Triangle, a square in Panama City, which forms part of the territory of the Zone. This step, however, did not satisfy the Panamanian aspirations, based on their interpretation of the Convention.

18. On June 13, 1962, Presidents Kennedy and Chiari issued a joint communiqué stating that they had agreed that "their representatives will arrange for the flying of Panamanian flags in an appropriate way in the Canal Zone." Both flags were flown since October 12, 1962, at the Bridge of the Americas (Thatcher Ferry Bridge), and since the end of that month at the Administration Buildings at Balboa Heights (Panama City) and Cristóbal (Colón). In the meantime, the Joint Commission, created by the two governments in pursuance of the communiqué of Presidents Kennedy and Chiari dated June 13, 1962, reached an agreement on January 10, 1963. Under this agreement both flags were to be flown on land in the Canal Zone wherever the flag of the United States was flown by civilian authorities. This agreement, however, was not immediately executed. According to the United States, the delay in the implementation of the agreement was mainly due to the United States authorities awaiting a judicial decision on the constitutionality of the "dual-

flags" accord. The time for an appeal against the decision, which was given on July 8, 1963, and which dismissed the complaints, expired on September 27, 1963, without an appeal having been filed.

19. It was only at this time that the Governor of the Canal Zone took action on the footing of the agreement. But he did not implement the agreement in such a way that the Panama flag was to be flown alongside the United States flag at every place where the United States flag had been flown, on January 10, 1963. Instead, the Governor selected seventeen spots where both flags were to be displayed. In other places, where the United States flag hitherto used to be flown, it was taken down by the Governor's orders on December 30, 1963. Especially with regard to schools, the Governor ordered that, though in front of the building no United States flag was to be flown, it was "in accordance with law and customs requiring the United States flag to be displayed in or near schools," for the United States flag to continue to be displayed in classrooms or elsewhere within the schools as at present.

20. This method of implementing the agreement between the two Presidents satisfied neither the Panamanian population nor the American inhabitants of the Canal Zone. The Panamanians were resentful that the Panamanian flag was not hoisted alongside the United States flag at all the places where the United States flag had been previously flown on land by the civilian authorities. The Americans in the Zone, on the other hand, did not easily accept the removal of their flag from the front of the schools where, according to American custom, it was usually flown.

21. When, after Christmas Holidays, schools in the Zone reopened on January 2, 1964, the United States flag, which used to fly in front of Balboa High School, in the part of the Zone nearest to Panama City, was no longer there; some four to five hundred students of the school sent a protest to President Johnson. On January 7, 1964, before classes had started, a number of students succeeded in raising the United States flag, notwithstanding the fact that the halyards on the pole had been locked. The Canal Zone Government and school authorities lowered the flag the same morning; subsequently on the same morning, at the end of the first class period, the flag was again hoisted by the students. This time a group of students posted themselves around the flag-pole in order to prevent the authorities from lowering the flag. After school, about 25 students remained on watch all night and were supplied with food and blankets by sympathizers. In the evening the flag was lowered and next morning it was raised again by the students. The school and civil authorities did not intervene. The Governor of the Canal Zone, however, issued a statement on January 8, 1964, in which he requested the cooperation of all United States citizens in honouring their country's commitments regardless of their personal beliefs. The next day, January 9, 1964,

the Governor broadcast a new statement on the flag issue. He then left the Zone for the United States in the afternoon of the same day.

Part III

FLAG INCIDENT OF JANUARY 9, 1964

22. As soon as the news about the Balboa High School flag incidents spread in Panama City, students of the Panamanian National Institute planned counteraction. On January 8, 1964, a Panamanian student-leader, Mr. Guillermo Guevara Pas, along with two other Panamanian students, went to the Balboa High School, saw the Principal and asked him questions about the flag. The Headmaster referred him to the Panama Canal Information Officer, Mr. Baldwin, with whom he then talked. Mr. Guevara Pas did not announce to the Principal or to Mr. Baldwin that he and his co-students planned a demonstration before the Balboa High School on the next day.

23. On the next day, January 9, 1964, after classes at about 4.45 p.m., a group of approximately 200 students left the Panamanian National Institute and marched into the Canal Zone by Gorgas Road. They carried a Panamanian flag, the banner of their organization, and placards. This march appears to have been very carefully prepared and did not appear to have been a spontaneous movement by the students. The flag they were carrying was that of the Panamanian National Institute; the Headmaster of the Institute gave them the flag for the purpose of a demonstration in front of the Balboa High School, without ascertaining whether the students had the permission of the School or the Canal Zone authorities to make the demonstration. The students were accompanied by photographers and film operators and before they had returned to the territory of the Republic of Panama, the news of their demonstration had spread among the population and a crowd was already waiting for their return in the streets near the frontier of the Canal Zone. The fact that a delegation of the students was received, immediately after their return, by the President of the Republic of Panama suggests that the Panamanian authorities may have had prior knowledge of the students' demonstration. In any case, the Ministry of External Affairs was informed by the students of their proposed demonstration before they took off.

24. It is beyond doubt that the march of the students, dressed in uniform, into the Canal Zone commenced in a peaceful and orderly manner. However, the students carried placards advising Governor Fleming to go home and claiming exclusive sovereignty over the Canal Zone for Panama.

25. Having passed the Administration Building of the Zone, the students were stopped by the head of the Canal Zone police in the

69

Balboa District, Captain Gaddis Wall. He asked them their plans and the students already mentioned, Mr. Guillermo Guevara Pas, told him that they intended to display the Panamanian flag at the flagpole of the Balboa High School and to sing their national anthem there. Captain Wall, speaking in English to the group of students through an interpreter, refused to let the procession approach the flagpole in front of the school, but proposed that a delegation of five students should display the Panamanian flag at the foot of the flagpole by holding it in their hands and sing the national anthem; they would not be allowed to hoist the flag on the flagpole. The rest of the students were required to remain on the opposite side of Gorgona Road, separated by the police from the American students and adults, and from the delegation with the flag.

26. In making his proposal, Captain Wall assured the students that their delegation would have complete protection and that they need not worry about their safety. The Panamanian students then had a discussion as to whether they would accept the proposal made by Captain Wall or not. After about 45 minutes deliberation among themselves, Mr. Guevara Pas informed Captain Wall that they were willing to accept his proposition. Accordingly, five students, four holding the flag and one the banner, crossed Gorgona Road and followed Captain Wall towards the School. A sixth student carrying a placard saying that Panama alone was sovereign in the Canal Zone joined the group that was accompanied by some policemen.

27. Having regard to the fact that interpreters had to be used, the general state of agitation of those concerned, and the length of the argument, the possibility cannot be excluded that the students had misunderstood Captain Wall's proposal; they may have understood it to mean that they had permission to hoist the Panamanian flag alongside the United States flag on the flagpole, rather than a mere display of the flag by holding it in their hands at the foot of the pole.

28. When the six students with Captain Wall arrived at the low hedge which surrounds the flagpole, some of the students started arguing and insisting that the Panamanian flag must be raised on the flagpole alongside the United States flag that was already flying. The flagpole had two sets of string which could have permitted the hoisting of two flags, but, according to Captain Wall, he had received orders to refuse to permit the hoisting of the Panamanian flag. After a few minutes of heated discussion, the group of six students, surrounded by a police cordon, proceeded over the hedge to the flagpole.

29. In the meantime, some 400 to 500 American students and adults had gathered in front of the school. A ring of American students surrounded the base of the flagpole inside the hedge. The Americans did not, in the words of Captain Wall, "behave entirely as I had hoped they would". The Balboa School students, as well as the adults,

appear to have expressed their protest against the Panamanian demonstration somewhat vigorously. As the Panamanian students approached the flagpole, the crowd of Balboa School students and adults started to sing the United States national anthem. This appears to have worsened the situation. At this stage, the Panamanian delegation was completely surrounded by the Americans.

30. Captain Wall, who had negotiated with the Panamanian students, did not at this time seriously try to calm the American students and adults. There is no indication that he, or any other person in authority, present, or near-by, tried to persuade the Americans to behave quietly when the Panamanian flag was displayed. Nor did anybody explain to them that the demonstration was directed against the flying of the American flag *alone* in front of the Balboa High School, contrary to the agreements between the two governments and contrary to the orders of the Governor of the Canal Zone.

31. Somewhere at about this stage, Captain Wall made a decision to cancel the Panamanian students' demonstration. He asked the Panamanian students to withdraw but they insisted on displaying the flag and singing their national anthem. The Panamanian students accused Captain Wall of not keeping his word and refused to withdraw. The main group of Panamanian students were still on the other side of Gorgona Road, separated from the delegation of six students by a line of police. Captain Wall ordered the police, who had followed the delegation, to hold their batons in front and physically to move the six Panamanian students back to the main group. The police then moved forward, urging the delegation to go to the other side of Gorgona Road. American students, also within the area which was surrounded by the hedge around the flagpole, mixed with the police and a crowd was formed, with the Panamanian students in the centre. The Panamanian students, who were bearing the Panamanian flag, were exposed to considerable stress, especially when two of them stumbled over the hedge and when, some 25 feet further, some fell a second time. At a certain stage in the general melée the Panamanian flag was torn. It was not proved that the flag was torn on purpose by American adults or students, nor was it proved that the flag was slightly torn before the six students proceeded to the flagpole with Captain Wall. It is quite likely that the flag, made of silk, was not able to resist the stress and strain of the occasion.

32. The delegation of Panamanian students was forced back by the police equipped with special riot-control batons until they were with the main body of the Panamanian students behind the police line on the other side of Gorgona Road. It is doubtful that the police used their batons only by holding the batons in both hands in front of them to push the Panamanian delegation back. Some of the policemen seem to have used their batons in a more agressive manner

71

against the retreating Panamanian students. As soon as the other students, who had thus far been waiting on the other side of the road for the displaying of their flag, saw their fellow students being forced back by the police, they started shouting and otherwise demonstrating their dissatisfaction. Some stones were thrown at the police line and one hit a policeman's helmet and caused him a slight wound through his helmet.

33. The retreat of the 200 demonstrating Panamanian students then started at a rather quick tempo. Patrol cars of the police followed them. The cancelling of the demonstration, the retreat with a torn flag, the hostile behaviour of the Americans in front of the Balboa High School, as well as during the retreat of the students, and the lack of any effective attempt by the police to quieten the American students and adults, had apparently caused a certain panic and resentment among the Panamanian students. The procession split up into two groups, the smaller one returning along Roosevelt Avenue to the Curundu area, and the second and bigger one following Gorgas Road, the same way back as the students had come, to 4th of July Avenue. On their way back to Panama City the students following Gorgas Road caused considerable damage. They rolled garbage cans on the road, according to them, in order to slow down the patrol cars that followed them. They smashed windows and street lights. Just before leaving the Zone, they smashed the traffic-control lights in Kennedy Avenue. It was mentioned that, when the students had arrived at the Episcopal Cathedral of St. Luke, two reports were heard which could have been caused by gun-shots. However, there was no further evidence on this matter.

34. The main group of students left the Zone at 6.45 to 7 p.m. and went to the National Institute on the Panamanian side of 4th of July Avenue.

PART IV

DISTURBANCES IN PANAMA CITY

35. As mentioned, somehow, even before the Panamanian students reached the Panamanian border, the news of the flag incidents and of the torn flag had, as vividly expressed by some of the witnesses, "spread like wildfire through the City of Panama", and a large crowd had already gathered in Calle G, which is adjacent to 4th of July Avenue, at about 6.30 p.m. At this time the crowd that had gathered ran into several hundreds.

36. When the Panamanian students crossed from the Canal Zone into the Republic of Panama between 6.45 and 7.00 p.m., a series of acts of violence had already taken place. A number of cars had been turned over and burnt on 4th of July Avenue in the neighbourhood of the National Institute.

72

37. The crowd grew rapidly and within about half an hour there were several thousand people all along the border extending from the Balboa Road entrance to the Ancon railway station. The violence of the crowd increased; there were repeated attempts at several points all along the border to enter the Canal Zone territory with the object not only of planting Panamanian flags but also of setting fire to property and otherwise threatening public safety.

38. In the meantime, repeated attempts were made by the Canal Zone authorities to call to their aid the Guardia Nacional of Panama to take effective measures to control the violent crowd. Between 6.30 and 8.30 p.m., 7 or 8 telephone calls were made by the American authorities but no effective action was taken by the Guardia Nacional. On the contrary, the Guardia Nacional was purposely kept away from the trouble-spots in the City of Panama until early on January 13.

39. At the beginning, the Canal Zone Police Force of the Balboa district, which comprises a maximum of approximately 80 men, tried to hold back the violent crowd along the nearly two kilometres long border by using most of the tear-gas available to them, and later, when faced by a growing and attacking crowd, by raising their police revolvers. In view of the size of the mob and the small police force available to the Canal Zone Authorities, at about 8.00 p.m., the acting Governor of the Zone, Lieutenant Governor Parker, called on the Commanding Officer of the United States forces, General O'Meara. He reported to him that he was unable to hold the position much longer and to maintain law and order with the help of the Police and requested military assistance from the U.S. armed forces in the Canal Zone. Immediately, General O'Meara gave such assistance.

40. In an attempt to assuage the crowds, General O'Meara sent out a small aeroplane relaying appeals over a loud-speaker in both Spanish and English, enjoining residents on both sides of the border to return to their homes. It does appear that the aeroplane flew not only over the Canal Zone territory but also over a part of the adjacent territory of the Republic of Panama. In view of the purpose of the flight, this can hardly be treated as a serious incursion of the air space of the Panamanian Republic. On the other hand, there was no evidence before us that any attempts were made by the authorities of the Panamanian Republic to assuage, calm or otherwise control the crowds. Indeed, on the contrary, from the materials made available, it would appear that statements made through the radio and the television were of an inflammatory nature. Incendiary bombs, or "Molotov Cocktails", were used during the rioting. These must have been made for this purpose. When, where and by whom they were made was not disclosed to the Investigating Committee. The fact that these were made and used would indicate some degree of pre-meditation and planning.

73

41. The Investigating Committee treats below the events as they occurred in different areas of the limits between the Republic of Panama and the Canal Zone.

42. Between 7.00 to 7.30 p.m. on January 9, part of the crowd had moved into the neighborhood of the Ancon railway station and the Ancon laundry. At the point where Frangipani Street intersects Roosevelt Avenue, the crowd started to attack passing cars, to turn them over and to set them on fire. An attempt was also made to set the laundry on fire by pushing a car on fire into it, and by using "Molotov Cocktails". Another part of the crowd forced its way into the railway station and set about destroying the station and its contents. A small group of policemen under a sergeant endeavoured to control this situation. In order to prevent the crowd from entering the residential areas behind the laundry, the police took up a position immediately behind the laundry and the railway station. A small theatre between the laundry and the residential area was evacuated. From this position, the police, by using tear-gas, started to drive the crowd back. When the situation seemed to be more difficult to control, the sergeant ordered his men to use their pistols. The pistol fire was directed over the heads of the crowd and into the ground in front of the crowd, but a part of the fire seems to have been directed into the crowd.

43. At about 7.45 p.m., a student of the National Institute, Ascanio Arosamena, aged 20, was hit by a bullet from a police revolver; it entered his shoulder, penetrated the thorax and resulted in the death of the student. Other persons appear also to have been injured by the pistol fire on the same occasion. The firing itself, however, forced the crowd back. It has been alleged that during this time civilians from the Canal Zone were seen using firearms along with the police. The Investigating Committee, however, had no evidence before it either to support or contradict this allegation.

44. The fire in the Ancon laundry was extinguished within a short time. A few minutes before 9.00 p.m. the United States Army took over, relieving the Canal Zone police in this area. Subsequently, it would appear that there were no further incidents in this particular area.

45. After 7.00 p.m., not far from the National Institute and further west from the Institute along 4th of July Avenue, the crowds turned over and burned cars, threw rocks into the Canal Zone territory and caused other damage. They also attacked an iron fence on the slope along the Avenue protecting the Canal Zone. They succeeded in tearing down the fence at approximately 9.00 p.m. Within minutes, the milling crowd surged into the Canal Zone territory at a point near the residence of Federal District Judge Crowe. The slope at this point is rather steep. The few policemen who were stationed there

74

held the crowd back by throwing tear-gas bombs into the crowd. The crowd attacking the Judge's house was armed with rocks and "Molotov Cocktails"; several "Molotov Cocktails" hit the Judge's house which, being an old wooden house, was set on fire in several places. The crowd surged higher up the slope and reached the Judge's house. At this stage the police drove the crowd back by firing shots, with shotguns, over the heads of the crowd. It does not appear that anyone was injured by these shots. The police, with the help of the Canal Zone fire brigade, successfully put out the fire. An inspection of the house established that it had been fired at.

46. At about 9.30 p.m., the United States Army took over the protection of this area and no further incidents occurred. It is noteworthy that the Judge and his family abandoned the house the following morning.

47. On the evening of January 9, at about 8.00 p.m., a large crowd, of probably over a thousand persons, made a concerted effort to enter the Canal Zone from the region of El Chorrillo in Panama by Balboa Road. It would appear that some one hundred or more people succeeded in entering the Canal Zone approximately 700 yards on Balboa Road. From this point, the crowd was driven back by the Canal Zone police, in the first instance by tear-gas and, when the police appear to have run out of tear-gas, by revolver fire. It would appear that the use of firearms was the only method by which, at this stage, the limited number of policemen present could prevent the crowd from forcing its way into the Canal Zone. It would also appear to the Investigating Committee that the revolver fire was not entirely directed over the heads of the crowd or into the ground in front of the crowd, but that some of it was directed into the crowd causing casualties.

48. A young boy, Estanislao Orobio, 18 years old, was fatally wounded at some stage during the night of January 9 to 10 in this area. It is alleged that he was the victim of the Canal Zone police revolver fire in this area on the evening of the 9th, when he, along with other companions, was carrying a Panamanian flag. The Investigating Committee is not entirely satisfied with the evidence put forward with regard to the circumstances of the death of this boy. There is some confusion as to the time when he was wounded—he died on January 11—and as to the type of firearm which caused the injuries. Under the circumstances, the Committee finds it difficult to decide whether he was the victim of the Canal Zone Police revolver fire or of subsequent shooting by the United States Army, or wounded in some other way.

49. At about 10.30 p.m. on January 9, the United States Army took over the protection of this area. No further incidents were reported.

50.   The area of greatest violence and damage appears to have been the central part of the border line in the district of Shaler Triangle, the Legislative Palace and the Pan American Building on the Panama side, and the Hotel Tivoli on the Canal Zone side. When the Panamanian students were returning from their demonstration outside the Balboa High School, at about 7.00 p.m. on January 9, they were joined by a large crowd; together the students and the crowd started to destroy the traffic lights and street lights on 4th of July Avenue. At the time when the first acts of violence started, there was still quite a heavy late afternoon traffic on the avenue, and the crowd threw rocks at passing cars. The Canal Zone Police found it hard to control and to protect the traffic. Shortly after 7.00 p.m., the normal stream of traffic appeared to have ceased and the street was filled by a milling, agitated crowd. The Canal Zone police gave up trying to control the traffic and took up a position on the other side of 4th of July Avenue, on the slope just within the Canal Zone territory, behind the dividing fence, in order to prevent the crowd from climbing the hill and coming over the fence.

51.   Between 7.30 to 8.00 p.m., a large crowd assembled in President Kennedy Avenue and concentrated near the Pan American Building; it was estimated to run into several thousand people. Later, the crowd not only turned over and set fire to cars and broke street lights, but also started to break through doors and windows, and generally to loot and destroy shops and property in Panama City. Sections of the crowd directed their wrecking activities to shops in parts of Panama City along 4th of July Avenue and other streets close to it. Windows were smashed and doors were forced open. The rioting lasted late into the night and the crowd set on fire the Pan American Building, which burned out. Six persons—possibly looters—seem to have been trapped in the building, where their dead bodies were found next morning.

52.   The Hotel Tivoli is an old wooden house, situated behind the iron fence that runs along 4th of July Avenue. Part of the crowd approached the Hotel on several occasions on the evening of January 9 and started throwing "Molotov Cocktails" and rocks against this building, which at the time was occupied by a number of guests, among them women and children. The Canal Zone Police drove the crowd back by using tear-gas and appeared to have controlled the situation until about 8.30 p.m., when the United States Army took over control of this area.

53.   The United States troops took up a position along Kennedy Avenue from the Mary Knoll Convent to the Hotel Tivoli and from the Hotel Tivoli down to the Ancon laundry. The troops used armoured personnel cars. The troops deployed appear to have succeeded in containing the crowd and preventing it from penetrating further into the Canal Zone by using large quantities of tear-gas.

54. Later in the evening, about 10.00 to 10.30 p.m., the United States troops in the vicinity of the Hotel Tivoli were fired on from the Panamanian side, from different directions and from what appears to have been a variety of firearms. A good part of the fire appeared to come from the Pan American Building and from the Legislative Palace in the Republic of Panama. From the time the United States Army took over the command of the Canal Zone, General O'Meara appears to have given clear orders to the troops not to fire and not to use any firearms. Following repeated requests, when the fire from the Panamanian territory grew in volume and effectiveness, the General in command gave orders, at about 10.50 p.m. on January 9, to return the fire by shotgun fire, and to direct the fire against the men firing from the Panamanian side, in order to quell the snipers. The shotgun fire was limited to the use of No. 4 - No. 7/1½ bird shot.

55. The Hotel Tivoli and surrounding area appear to have been the main target for the firing from the Panamanian side during these days. The bullets recovered established that the weapons used from the Panamanian side included rifles, long and short revolvers and .38 automatics (9 mm.). On the Hotel Tivoli, the marks of no less than 465 bullets were found. It would appear that the calibres used there were .22 to .45 (5.5 mm. to 11.35 mm.) and that .22 calibre bullets predominated. There was evidence also that there were intermittent bursts of automatic or semi-automatic fire coming from the Panamanian side from about 12.30 a.m. until the early hours of the morning of the 10th. It should be mentioned that, in Panama City, looters forced their way into the shop of a dealer in firearms and looted weapons and ammunition.

56. A select team of United States Army marksmen under a sergeant was ordered to take up position in the Hotel Tivoli late in the evening of January 9. General O'Meara made at least two requests, through the appropriate Panamanian authorities, for action by the Panamanian authorities to stop the firing which was being directed against the Canal Zone from the Republic of Panama. No action having been taken by the Panamanian authorities, through the Guardia Nacional or otherwise, General O'Meara issued orders after midnight on January 10, that the team of U.S. Army marksmen could use .30 calibre rifle fire to stop the snipers. At this stage four U.S. soldiers had been wounded, making a total of six casualties on the U.S. side. One soldier and one civilian had been wounded earlier.

57. The rifle firing by the U.S. Army marksmen from the Hotel Tivoli commenced on the morning of the 10th at about 12.30 a.m., and continued until 2.00 to 3.00 a.m. the same day. It started again about 10.00 a.m. on the morning of the 10th, and continued until about 2.00 p.m. It was resumed again from 7.10 to 7.15 p.m. on the

same evening. It is estimated that some 400 to 500 bullets were fired by the United States forces. An examination of the Legislative Building showed that bullets had penetrated through the walls. Throughout this period U.S. troops also used shotguns intermittently.

58.   It was alleged that the United States Army used armoured tanks, but the Investigating Committee is satisfied from evidence before it that armoured personnel carriers using caterpillar tracks instead of wheels were mistaken for tanks. There was no evidence of any firing from tanks or armoured personnel carriers.

59.   In the area indicated above, in consequence of the fire from the Panamanian side, 10 soldiers of the United States Army were injured. On the Panamanian side the casualties appear to have been greater. A scrutiny of the records of St. Thomas's Hospital showed that a total of 95 injured persons were brought to this hospital. Of these, 18 were fatal; six of these appear to have died when trapped in the fire of the Pan American Building. Of the remaining twelve fatal casualities, in only six cases were the particulars presented to the Committee sufficient to enable an investigation into the circumstances of their deaths. These cases are dealt with later. As for the remaining six fatal cases, it is quite conceivable that, in view of the well directed high velocity rifle fire of the U.S. Army against snipers, some of them were snipers killed by U.S. Army fire, though the records of their deaths were not brought to the notice of the Investigating Committee. Under these circumstances the Investigating Committee found it impossible to establish with certainty the exact number of casualties on the Panamanian side caused by U.S. Army fire. Furthermore, Panamanians fired on each other, on different occasions, for different reasons. It seems also probable that shop-keepers and others used weapons in order to stop looting and to protect their property.

60.   Among the six cases presented to the Investigating Committee, two have already been dealt with. The other four cases are the following.

61.   An old fruiterer, Rogelio Lara, was killed by a rifle bullet on the evening of January 9, between 9.00-10.00 p.m., while lying or resting in the Avenida Central. It seems unlikely that this old man was killed by an American rifleman, because the evidence indicates that the death was not caused by a high velocity bullet such as used by the United States marksmen. At the time the man was hit there seems to have been no American fire in this area.

62.   Another man, Rodolfo Sanchez, aged 33, sitting in a car near the Casa Müller, was shot and killed shortly before noon of January 10. This would appear to have been caused by a .30 calibre rifle, such as was used by the United States marksmen. It is proved that the marksmen were shooting in this direction at this particular time.

63. A young girl, Rosa Elena Landecho, aged 11 was the unfortunate victim of a rifle bullet at about noon on January 10, when she was on the balcony of the flat of her family in the house No. 1 Calle M. In all probability, she was shot by a bullet from a marksman directed against a sniper in the same building. This conjecture is born out by the Committee's on-the-spot visit which indicated a spray of rifle bullets on this building. The medical evidence shows that it was not totally impossible, even if it were unlikely, that this girl was killed by a .30 calibre bullet such as used by the marksmen.

64. A taxi-driver, Victor Garibaldo, aged 29, died on the morning of January 10 from a wound inflicted by a .30 calibre rifle. He appears to have been somewhere close to the Legislative Palace, which was the area from which there was considerable firing from the Panamanian side, and was probably shot by a marksman's bullet.

65. During January 10-11, the crowd appears to have diminished greatly, but still about a thousand people moved to and fro in the streets. There was clear evidence that, on January 10 and 11, at several points a mob endeavoured to force an entry into the Canal Zone with the apparent purpose of destroying life and property. Shooting from the Panamanian side continued from January 11 to January 12. On the afternoon of January 10, the United States troops ceased to return the fire from the Panamanian side by rifle-fire, except for a very short period of some minutes during the evening. As a result of orders given by General O'Meara, the Panamanian fire was not returned by the United States Army afterwards. By the early morning of January 13, the Guardia Nacional appeared, took the situation in hand and restored order in the streets neighbouring the Canal Zone in the City of Panama. The Investigating Committee feels satisfied that, if the Guardia Nacional had taken charge of the situation early on the evening of the 9th or soon thereafter, the violence and the damage to property and the tragic casualties would not, in all probability, have taken place.

PART V

DISTURBANCES IN COLÓN

66. The news of the disturbances and violence in Panama City and on the border area between Panama City and the Canal Zone, spread rapidly to other parts of Panama including Cristóbal-Colón. In addition, the radio broadcasts from Panama City created a tense atmosphere in Colón.

67. At about 9.00 p.m. on the evening of January 9, a crowd of approximately 1,000 to 1,500 people entered from Colón into the Cristóbal area in the Canal Zone and proceeded down Roosevelt Avenue to the Panama Canal Administration Building in Cristóbal.

There was a reasonably peaceful demonstration, and the Mayor of Colón was present at the time of the demonstration. Some leaders of the crowd insisted on hoisting the Panamanian flag on the flagpoles in the Administration Building in Cristóbal. In the day-time, the Panamanian flag was normally hoisted at this place alongside and with the U.S. flag, but at this time in the evening both flags were usually lowered for the night. The Panamanian flag was, however, now raised again on its flagpole and flown without objection and the crowd was permitted to sing the Panamanian national anthem. After this ceremony the flag was lowered again by the demonstrators. It is noteworthy that the Canal Zone Authorities, including the local Chief of Police, Captain Howard, handled the crowds tactfully and with persuasion and restraint.

68. The demonstration over, the crowd returned to Colón. As the crowd moved away from Cristóbal, however, certain elements in the crowd damaged a car that was parked in Cristóbal by smashing its windows. In Colón the crowd then moved towards the American Consulate.

69. A little later the same evening, at about 9.45 p.m., a crowd of several thousand people started new demonstrations, a part of the crowd marching along Balboa Avenue into the Canal Zone between the Masonic Temple and the old Commissary. In the beginning, Captain Howard, who was in charge of the police in Cristóbal, appears to have successfully stopped the crowd some 10 yards inside the Canal Zone and dissuaded them from coming further forward on Balboa Road into the Canal Zone, by addressing them in Spanish. At about the same time, another crowd on the other side of the Masonic Temple in Bolivar Avenue started resorting to violence. They threw rocks and other objects, breaking windows of the Y.M.C.A. building and of the Masonic Temple. The tempo of violence appears to have increased rather quickly; the Canal Zone police, being outnumbered by the large crowds, called for U.S. Army assistance.

70. At about 10.30 p.m., troops of the United States Army took control of the situation in Cristóbal and in the area around the Masonic Temple, the Y.M.C.A. and the old Commissary. The United States troops arrived in battle uniform and helmets, guns held forward with fixed bayonets, and approached the crowd that had gathered on Balboa Avenue from the Colón side. By this time the crowd appears to have been very excited. Despite Captain Howard's attempts to persuade them to disperse and move away, a small, determined group on Balboa Avenue remainded defiant, heading further towards Cristóbal. The soldiers appear to have come right up to the small group standing their ground on Balboa Avenue; they stopped there in an attempt to make a show of force to persuade the crowd to move away. It is quite conceivable that this led to the Panamanians grabbing the bayonets and guns, thus starting a scuffle. In any event,

it is clear beyond doubt that, at this time, severe rioting continued in the immediate neighbourhood of the Masonic Temple and the Y.M.C.A., in the course of which two buildings were seriously damaged. Windows of shops were smashed open, and looting seems to have taken place.

71. At about 10.45 p.m. the crowd having been pushed back into the Republic of Panama, the officer commanding the U.S. troops posted soldiers all along the border between the Republic of Panama and the Canal Zone, in 11th Street and Bolivar Avenue, in order to seal off the Canal Zone. At about this time, one of the U.S. officers in charge of a platoon inadvertently led a small number of his men in Bolivar Avenue over the line forming the border between the Canal Zone and the Republic of Panama to a point which was a few yards within the Republic of Panama. This error appears to have been corrected within a matter of minutes by a superior officer.

72. The crowd opposite the soldiers became violent and at about 11.45 p.m. one of the U.S. soldiers was wounded by a shot. A little later, shortly after midnight, a U.S. soldier was killed by a bullet fired from the crowd at a soldier standing on duty. Up to this time the U.S. soldiers stood without any protection and used only tear-gas to disperse the crowd and prevent it from entering the Canal Zone. In view of the casualties suffered, the soldiers were moved back into the Y.M.C.A. building, the Masonic Temple and the old Commissary, just inside the Canal Zone, to afford them protection.

73. Early on the morning of the 10th, two more U.S. soldiers were shot dead by bullets fired from the Canal Zone, and nine others were wounded. Through the night and early morning, the violence appears to have continued; it reached a new peak at 10.00 a.m., when "Molotov Cocktails" thrown against the Y.M.C.A. building at last set it on fire and burned it down. The Masonic Temple and the old Commissary were also attacked with rocks and "Molotov Cocktails". The old Commissary was set on fire at noon the next day, the 11th, and was also burned down.

74. From the evening of the 9th and through the days and nights of the 10th, 11th and 12th, the American troops were kept under fire from different points in the Republic of Panama. It was only on the afternoon of the 11th, at about 2.45 p.m., that General O'Meara gave permission to the local commander to use shotguns in order to counter the firing from the Republic of Panama. By this time, three U.S. soldiers had been killed and twelve had been wounded by the fire from the Panamanian side.

75. In the early hours of the morning of the 12th, about 2.00 a.m., a jeep of the Guardia Nacional was driven up 11th Street heading west, towards the harbour. It got entangled in some barbed wire at the corner of 11th Street and Balboa Avenue and came to a halt.

The car had its headlamps on facing towards the barbour; otherwise the area was in complete darkness, the street lights having been shot out. A sergeant of the Guardia named Celestino Villareta, 43 years old, sitting next to the driver in the jeep, was shot dead at this moment by a bullet. It is clear that the jeep received fire from two sides: shotgun fire from behind the top of the Masonic Temple by the United States troops and rifle fire in the front from the direction of the harbour; if from inside or outside the Canal Zone was not clarified. At no time did the United States troops use bullet fire in Colón and the wound that caused the death of the Guardia Sergeant clearly was caused by a bullet. This bullet must have come either from a rifle fired by a United States soldier against orders or from some unknown sniper. It was established that after the jeep had been fired on, the U.S. Colonel in charge was requested over the telephone by an officer of the Guardia to order the United States troops to stop firing while an ambulance was being sent to pick up the body of the Guardia Sergeant, and another man who was wounded in the jeep. The Colonel agreed to this and gave specific orders to his men to withold fire when the ambulance approached the jeep. Nevertheless, fire appears to have been opened on the ambulance from the same direction—the harbour—by an unidentified person.

76. A six-month old infant, Maritza Avila Alabarea, was reported to have died in Colón as a consequence of the effects of tear-gas. Though the Investigating Committee requested evidence with regard to this unfortunate death, none was made available. It was therefore impossible for the Committee to reach any conclusion regarding the circumstance under which the child died.

77. Although the United States troops used shotguns to counter the fire from the Panamanian side from some time on the afternoon of January 11th until the morning of the 13th, no evidence was submitted to the Investigating Committee of any deaths having been caused by shotgun fire. Thirteen persons, however, were reported to have been wounded or injured by shotgun fire in Colón.

78. The Investigating Committee was satisfied on the evidence that, from time to time, the U.S. Army and police officials of the Canal Zone were in communication with the officials of the Guardia, who appear to have cooperated and endeavoured, within their limits, to restore order. Curiously, it was also proved that the Guardia were totally disarmed during these difficult days; the Guardia are usually equipped with pistols and batons. No explanation was given as to why the Guardia were ordered not to carry their usual arms during these days.

79. Nevertheless, the Guardia brought the situation completely under control on the morning of the 13th; this coincided with similar effective action taken by the Guardia in Panama City.

PART VI

RESTRICTIONS IN COLÓN CORRIDOR
AND ON THE BRIDGE

80. The City of Colón, which is under Panamanian jurisdiction, is on all sides surrounded by the Canal Zone. However, the Trans-Isthmian Highway leading from Panama City to Colón is under Panamanian jurisdiction, forming in part a Corridor approximately four miles long running from the Canal Zone border, nearby to the town of Kativa, to the City of Colón. It was alleged that the United States authorities through their armed forces, blocked and closed the Colón Corridor.

81. In December 1963, the Panamanian authorities closed the Corridor to vehicular traffic in view of reconstruction work on the road within the Corridor. All the normal traffic to Colón therefore passed, not through the Corridor, but through another road in the Canal Zone territory, Randolph Road and Bolívar Highway.

82. On the night of January 9th, after the disturbances started and the United States armed forces had taken over control, a check-point was established on the Bolívar Highway, within the Canal Zone, to prevent armed infiltration into the Zone. The purpose of this check-point was to search suspects and to ensure that no one entered the area with weapons; very few people were stopped and some were found with weapons—they were prevented from passing this check-point. No vehicular traffic bearing supplies or goods was prevented from passing this check-point by the United States forces; there was no evidence that any governmental official or other responsible persons were stopped from passing the check-point.

83. On January 10th, in the early hours of the morning, the United States forces established an additional check-point at the end of the Colón Corridor where it enters Central Avenue within the Canal Zone limit, partly inside Panamanian territory. The purpose of this check-point was also restricted to preventing persons entering with weapons and it only screened pedestrian traffic, as the road was closed to vehicular traffic. No person appears to have been stopped from passing this check-point. It was established that, before this check-point was established outside the Colón Corridor, the United States military authorities had asked the Guardia Nacional to establish a similar check-point in order to screen the traffic. On the afternoon of the 11th, at 2.45 p.m., this check-point was taken over by the Guardia Nacional. Soon after the United States armed forces had established its check-point on the evening of the 10th at the end of the Colón Corridor, certain private individuals (probably Panamanians) set up a check-point further up on Bolívar Highway in the

Canal Zone, so that, all traffic coming from Colón reaching the United States Army check-point necessarily had to go through this private check-point where the traffic was halted and searched. The Canal Zone authorities appear to have exercised restraint in not interfering with this check-point, which was within the Canal Zone.

84. The Bridge of the Americas (Thatcher Ferry Bridge), after the outbreak of the disturbances on the evening of January 9th, was put under strict control by the armed forces of the United States. During night-time, for the three nights beginning on January 9th, all traffic was completely closed except for official and what was described as "emergency" traffic, such as, the Guardia Nacional, doctors, nurses, blood supplies, etc. Subject to a check and inspection, the bridge was open to all traffic during the daytime from the early morning of January 10th. The bridge is situated within the Canal Zone and was constructed and is owned by the United States. It is admitted that the bridge is under the exclusive jurisdiction and control of the United States. The Republic of Panama has complete and free right of way over the bridge, as it has over all public roads of the Canal Zone, by virtue of the provisions of the Convention of 1903.

PART VII

CONCLUSIONS

A. *General*

85. In the course of our work a number of problems of international law have arisen, such as, the interpretation of the Convention of 1903, other Conventions between the United States and the Republic of Panama, legal aspects of shooting from one territory into another, violations of national territory, the right of peaceful assembly of citizens of one territory in another territory, and a number of other questions involving the interpretation or definition of particular international and/or municipal laws which might be applicable to the situation. We do not think it is our function to deal with or decide these problems.

86. The issues to be decided by us depend on questions of fact and on the proper interpretation of the Universal Declaration of Human Rights, and its implications. We have endeavoured in the conclusions reached to construe the relevant Articles of the Universal Declaration of Human Rights in accordance with the accepted principles relating to such Articles, the principles of natural justice, the generally recognized concepts of the Rule of Law, and good common sense. In doing so we have also carefully considered the relevant Articles of the European Convention on Human Rights, of the Inter-American Draft Convention on Human Rights, as well as the relevant provisions contained in national constitutions.

B. *Article 3 of the Universal Declaration of Human Rights*

87. Article 3 of the Universal Declaration of Human Rights provides that:

> "Everyone has the right to life, liberty and security of person."

88. The allegation we were asked to investigate was that the United States had violated this Article. On the facts proved before us, we are unable to come to this conclusion.

89. Undoubtedly there was, as a result of the firing by the United States armed forces, a tragic loss of life on the Panamanian side. It must be recognized that in all civilized communities such an absolute right, as is enshrined in Article 3, would not exclude certain necessary and reasonable exceptions. Thus, it would not be a contravention of Article 3 to deprive a person of life, liberty and security of person in order to prevent injury to other persons from unlawful violence and in order to quell a riot or violent disturbance, provided, however, that the force used was not more than that absolutely necessary. The necessary minimum force may include the use of firearms.

90. The tempo and violence of the disturbances were such that there is little doubt that they held out a real threat to life and security, which could only be met by strong measures. In these circumstances the Canal Zone Authorities and the United States military forces were entitled to use force. Nevertheless, we entertained some doubts as to whether the force used, at some stages, was not in excess of the minimum absolutely necessary. In particular the following caused us concern:

1. In regard to the shooting by the Canal Zone police with revolvers during the early part of the evening of January 9th, we are concerned with the following matters:

    (*a*) While the Canal Zone Police had exhausted the greater part of the tear-gas available to them, it was established that they did not try to obtain additional supplies.

    (*b*) No attempt appears to have been made to use water jets to calm down and control the crowd.

    (*c*) It also appears that, while orders were given to shoot over the heads of people or into the ground in front of the crowd, people in the crowd were struck by bullets which did not appear to be "ricochet" bullets.

2. A large number of bullets (approximately 400-500) were fired by United States Army trained marksmen using high velocity rifles.

In a residential and densely populated area such extensive use of high fire-power is a disturbing feature.

3. The exercise and show of force by United States Army personnel by marching in full battle kit right up to a crowd in Colón, with guns mounted with bayonets drawn in a position of attack.

91. While these matters have caused us concern we have to take into account *all* the surrounding circumstances and in particular the following:

Revolver Fire (See [1] above)

    (a) The comparatively small number of Canal Zone Police (75-80).

    (b) The large dimensions and violent temper of the crowds.

    (c) The deliberate and extensive use of incendiaries ("Molotov Cocktails").

    (d) The failure of the Panamanian authorities and of the Guardia Nacional to take effective steps to control the crowd and maintain order within the territory of the Republic of Panama.

Rifle Fire (See [2] above)

    (a) The heavy firing from the Panamanian side, by a variety of weapons, running into hundreds of bullets (estimated close to 1,000).

    (b) The fact that the United States Army did not order firing by rifles until it had sustained several casualities as a result of the firing from the Panamanian territory.

    (c) The failure of the Panamanian authorities and of the Guardia Nacional to remove snipers and other elements using firearms within Panamanian territory directed against the Canal Zone.

Use of Bayonets (See [3] above)

    (a) A large and threatening crowd had gathered and a section of the crowd had started causing destruction and damage.

    (b) The show of force could have been considered an effective means of dispersing the crowd.

    (c) The failure of the Guardia Nacional to maintain order, to disperse the crowd and to prevent unlawful acts of violence.

92. Considering all the above surrounding circumstances, and in particular the grave acts of violence and the threat to life and security involved, we have come to the conclusion that, even if the force used by the Canal Zone Authorities and the United States Army may have been at certain stages somewhat in excess of what was absolutely necessary at the time, the force used seems to have been justified; taking into account such rapidly moving, critical, and violent conditions, it is impossible to lay down a fine distinguishing line of what should have been the absolute minimum necessary.

93. We regret deeply that the Panamanian authorities made no attempt during the critical early hours, as well as for almost three days thereafter, to curb and control the violent activities of the milling crowds. On the contrary, there is considerable evidence to indicate that broadcasts over radio, television and loud-speakers, newspapers, and other means were adopted to incite and misinform the Panamanian public without any action by the Panamanian authorities to curtail or moderate such activities.

C. *Article 5 of the Universal Declaration of Human Rights*

94. Article 5 of the Universal Declaration of Human Rights provides that:

> "No one shall be subjected to torture or to cruel, inhuman or degrading treatment or punishment."

95. The allegation we were asked to investigate under this heading was that the United States had violated this Article by reason of the action of the Canal Zone Police and of the United States armed forces in shooting at the Panamanian civil population. As set out in detail in Part II, the occasions when shooting was resorted to by the Canal Zone police or United States Army were: (1) revolver fire by Canal Zone police to prevent the crowds from surging forward and coming further into the Canal Zone, when it was patent that the purpose of these crowds was to commit unlawful acts of violence; (2) rifle shots by trained marksmen of the United States Army to silence the snipers on the Panamanian side and thus to prevent further casualties to the United States armed personnel as well as civilians; (3) firing of bird-shot to repel violent crowds from forcing an entry into the Canal Zone and also to silence snipers; and (4) shooting in order to put out the street lights.

96. We doubt if this Article was intended to deal with situations such as those under review. Article 5 appears to us to have been intended to deal with cases of persons who have already lost their liberty, or who are being subjected to endemic ill-treatment, rather than to deal with a temporary, emergency situation.

97. However, even if this be incorrect, it appears to us that the issues involved here are identical to those already dealt with in regard to the allegation of a violation of Article 3. Accordingly, on the basis of the same reasoning adopted by us in regard to our previous conclusion we do not accept the allegation that the United States violated Article 5.

D. *Article 20 of the Universal Declaration of Human Rights*

98. The allegation of the National Bar Association of Panama under this head was of a breach by the United States of Article 20 of the Universal Declaration of Human Rights. However, we take it that the allegation is in fact limited to Sub-Article (1) of Article 20; Sub-Article (2) does not seem to have any relevance to the matters under investigation.

99. Article 20 (1) provides that:

"Everyone has the right to freedom of peaceful assembly and association."

100. It is universally accepted that such an absolute right as is granted by Article 20 (1) must necessarily be curtailed in even the freest and most democratic society to meet the interests of national security, or public safety, or for the prevention of disorder, violence or crime, or for the protection of rights and freedoms of others.

101. We would here refer to the Inter-American Draft Convention on Human Rights, Article 12 whereof provides:

"The right of peaceful assembly, without arms, is recognized. No restrictions may be placed on the exercise of this right other than those imposed in conformity with the law and necessary in a democratic society in the interest of national security, public safety or public order, or for the protection of public health or morals, or of the rights and freedom of others."

102. Similar provisions delimiting the right of free assembly are contained in most national constitutions, including the Constitution of Panama.

103. The facts and background with regard to the flag incident and the demonstration by the students of the National Institute of Panama on the afternoon of January 9th at the Balboa High School in the Canal Zone have been set out in some detail in Part I.

104. In view of the turn events took, we are unable to come to a conclusion that there was a violation of the right of assembly as guaranteed in Article 20 (1), for the reason that the Canal Zone

88

police were entitled to use force and disperse the assembly to prevent disorder and an outbreak of violence.

105. We cannot, however, help feeling that the Canal Zone authorities, and in particular the Canal Zone police, could have handled the situation with greater foresight. The Panamanian students having been permitted to stage their demonstration and march into the compound of the Balboa School, and the police captain having assured the safe conduct of the small group of Panamanian students who were to carry out their flag demonstration and sing the Panamanian national anthem, we think that the Panamanian students should have been better protected, and that the provocative acts of the United States students and citizens should have been more firmly handled. It was particularly unfortunate that physical force, by the use of batons on the Panamanian students who had been previously assured safe conduct, was not avoided.

106. We would also observe that it is patent that under the charged atmosphere of the area, the flag had become a special symbol for the Panamanians as well as the citizens of the United States, particularly the students. In this atmosphere, and in the light of the accord reached in June 1962 between Presidents Kennedy and Chiari, we find it difficult to understand why the Canal Zone authorities, including the Balboa School authorities, did not take firmer and stronger action to implement the flag agreement with regard to their own students.

107. With regard to the allegation that the right of assembly was violated on January 9th, 10th and 11th by reason of the actions of the Canal Zone police and of the United States armed forces in firing small arms and in using tear-gas for the purpose of preventing such right of assembly inside the Republic of Panama, we do not accept that there was any such violation because the crowds against whom such measures were taken were not peaceful but were violent and posed an immediate threat to public safety.

E. *Article 13 (1) of the Universal Declaration of Human Rights*

108. Sub-Article (1) of Article 13 of the Universal Declaration of Human Rights provides that:

"Everyone has the right to freedom of movement and residence within the borders of each state."

109. The Panamanian allegation of "blockade" implies that by reason of the control exercised by the United States Army over the Colón Corridor and the Bridge of the Americas (Thatcher Ferry Bridge) Article 13 (1) of the Universal Declaration was violated. We do not find this allegation proved.

89

110.   Insofar as the Colón Corridor is concerned, it was proved that in the early hours of the morning of January 10th, the United States armed forces established a check-point at the end of the Colón Corridor where it enters Central Avenue within the Canal Zone limit. The purpose of this check-point was to ensure that persons in possession of weapons and firearms did not go through, and it would appear that no person was stopped from passing the check-point. The establishment of such a check-point in itself does not, in our opinion, constitute an infringement of freedom of movement as guaranteed by Artible 13 (1) of the Universal Declaration of Human Rights.

111.   For some time at night all traffic over the Bridge of the Americas (Thatcher Ferry Bridge) appears to have been completely closed except for some official traffic. There was also imposed at both ends of the Bridge a check and inspection to screen the traffic. This does constitute a restriction on the free movement of traffic. The closing of traffic at night caused inconvenience and even hardship in respect of commercial traffic carrying supplies and commodities transported at night, such as milk, etc. In view, however, of all the surrounding circumstances, particularly the importance of ensuring the security and safety of the Bridge and of the traffic over it, we are of the opinion that this restriction was in the nature of control during an emergency and was such as did not amount to an infringement of the right of freedom of movement contemplated by Article 13 (1).

F.   *Inequality of Treatment*

112.   Regarding the alleged inequality of treatment in the Canal Zone, we are unable, on the basis of the limited materials placed before us, to reach a specific conclusion. We feel, however, that we should convey certain clear impressions we have formed.

113.   Since the construction of the Canal, separate communities have lived on two sides of what is known as the Canal Zone border. On the one side United States citizens in the Canal Zone, and on the other Panamanians in the Republic of Panama. Over the years it has given rise to a divergency in the way of life, in the economy, and in the outlook of the two peoples living in close proximity and yet in virtual isolation from each other. It is unfortunate that the United States citizens who have lived all their lives in the Canal Zone, and, perhaps more particularly, the second and third generation United States citizens who were born and raised in the Canal Zone, have developed a particular state of mind not conducive to the promotion of happier relations between them and the people of Panama. Indeed, on the contrary, this particular state of mind has resulted in building up resentment over the decades which has found expression in the type of unbalanced attitudes on both sides such as on the subject of flying their respective flags, as was demonstrated during the un-

fortunate days covered by this report, and also for some considerable time previously. The passage of time, instead of assuaging these conflicting tendencies, appears to have aggravated them. Tension and resentment have increased in a vicious circle and have not been improved by certain reactions of the Panamanians.

114. We cannot help feeling that the United States, having regard to the special situation it occupies in the world, and with its resources and ideals, should reflect upon these sad facts and take effective steps to make possible a reorientation and change in the outlook and thinking of the people living in the Canal Zone. Undoubtedly this is a difficult and uphill task but it would yield rich dividends in healthier relations with the people of Panama. The Government of Panama and the life and economy of Panama is in many ways so closely tied to the Panama Canal that it would not be out of place to suggest that the Panamanian Government and Panamanian people should also reflect upon the facts as they appear to impartial observers and should exercise tolerance, moderation and understanding in their relations with the United States and Canal Zone authorities.

115. In conclusion we express the fervent hope that in some small measure our work will contribute to the growth of understanding, cooperation and amity between the two countries and their peoples, so that they may move forward in the furtherance of their mutual vital interests.

A. D. BELINFANTE
GUSTAF PETRÉN
NAVROZ VAKIL

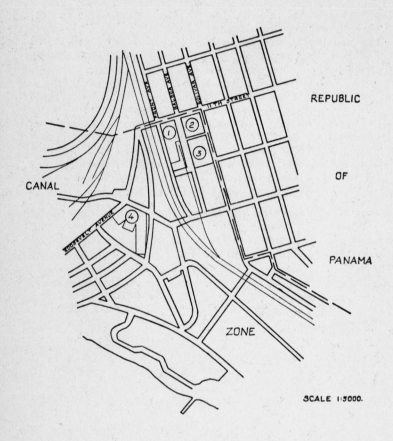

REPUBLIC

OF

PANAMA

CANAL

ZONE

SCALE 1:5000.

1. Commissary
2. Masonic Temple
3. Y.M.C.A. Building
4. Panama Canal Administration Building

—— — —— Republic of Panama - Canal Zone Boundary

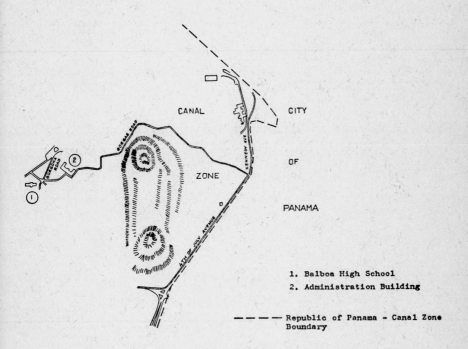

CANAL

CITY

OF

PANAMA

ZONE

1. Balboa High School

2. Administration Building

— — — — Republic of Panama - Canal Zone
Boundary

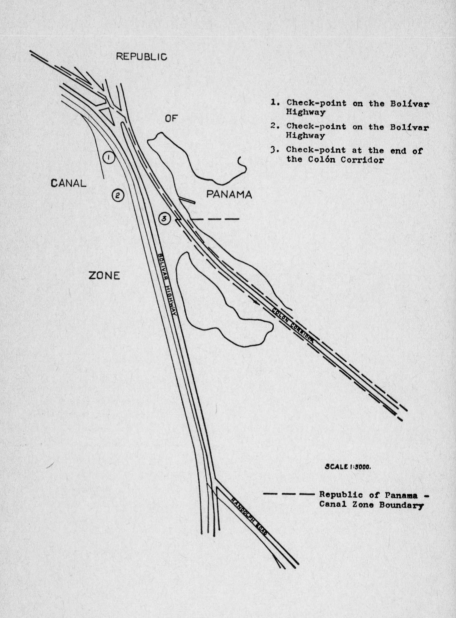

REPUBLIC

OF

PANAMA

CANAL

ZONE

BOLIVAR HIGHWAY

COLON CORRIDOR

RANDOLPH ROAD

1. Check-point on the Bolívar Highway
2. Check-point on the Bolívar Highway
3. Check-point at the end of the Colón Corridor

SCALE 1:5000.

——— Republic of Panama –
         Canal Zone Boundary

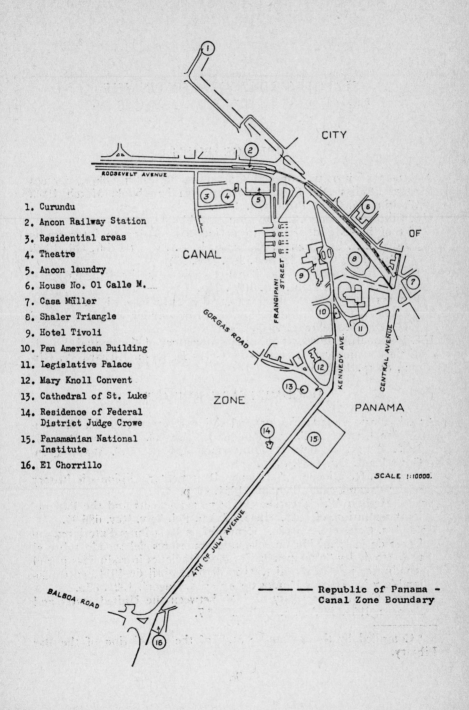

CITY

OF

CANAL

PANAMA

ZONE

ROOSEVELT AVENUE

FRANGIPANI STREET

GORGAS ROAD

KENNEDY AVE.

CENTRAL AVENUE

4TH OF JULY AVENUE

BALBOA ROAD

1. Curundu
2. Ancon Railway Station
3. Residential areas
4. Theatre
5. Ancon laundry
6. House No. 01 Calle M.
7. Casa Müller
8. Shaler Triangle
9. Hotel Tivoli
10. Pan American Building
11. Legislative Palace
12. Mary Knoll Convent
13. Cathedral of St. Luke
14. Residence of Federal
    District Judge Crowe
15. Panamanian National
    Institute
16. El Chorrillo

SCALE 1:10000.

—— —— —— Republic of Panama -
Canal Zone Boundary

SELECTED BIBLIOGRAPHY ON THE LEGAL AND HISTORICAL ASPECTS OF THE PANAMA CANAL*

BIBLIOGRAPHIES

American University. Special Operations Research Office. Foreign Areas Studies Div. Special warfare area handbook. March 1962. Washington, Gov't Print. Off. 488p.

U.S. Library of Congress. Division of Bibliography.
List of books and articles in periodicals relating to interoceanic canals . . . by Hugh A. Morrison, jr. . . . Gov't Print. Off. 1900. 174p. (56th Cong., 1st Sess. Sen. Doc. 59)
List of references on the Panama canal and the Panama canal zone . . . Gov't Print. Off. 1919. 21p.
Panama canal and the Panama canal zone, a selected list of references compiled by Ann Duncan Brown under the direction of Florence S. Hellman. 1943. 57p.

U.S. National Archives. Preliminary inventory of the textual records of the Panama canal; revised by Garry D. Ryan. Richard W. Giroux, comp. 1963. 36p.

DOCUMENTARY SOURCES

American and Panamanian general claims arbitration under the convention between U.S. and Panama of July 28, 1926 and Dec. 17, 1932. Report of Bert L. Hunt, agent for the U.S. Washington, Gov't Print. Off. 1934. 872p.

Arosemena, G., Diogenes A., comp. Documentary diplomatic history of the Panama canal. Panama, 1961. 496p.

Briggs, Herbert W. Treaties, executive agreements and the Panama joint resolution. of 1943. 1943. 37 Am. Pol. Serv. Rev. 686-91.

Colombia. Congreso. Senado. Comisión de Relaciones Exteriores. Informe de la Comisión de relaciones exteriores del senado sobre el proyecto de ley "que aprueba las modificaciones introducidas por el senado norteamericano al tratado de 6 de abril de 1914" entre Colombia y los Estados Unidos de América. Bogotá. 1921. 88p.

Fenwick, C. G. The treaty of 1955 between the United States and Panama. 1955. 49 Am. J. Int'l L. 543-7.

---

*Compiled by the Reference Staff of the Association of the Bar Library.

Panama canal company and canal zone government annual report. 1951. Washington, D.C.

The Panama Canal. Treaties and acts of congress relating to the isthmian canal. Washington, Gov't Print. Off. 1914. 58p.

Sullivan and Cromwell, comp. Compilation of executive documents and diplomatic correspondence relative to a trans-isthmian canal in Central America. With specific reference to the treaty of 1846 between the United States and New Granada (U.S. of Colombia) and the "Clayton-Bulwer" treaty of 1850 between the U.S. and Great Britain . . . New York, Evening Post Job Printing House. 1905. 3v.

Treaty between Great Britain and the United States to facilitate the construction of a ship canal (Hay-Pauncefote treaty) concluded Nov. 18, 1901. 1909. 3 Am. J. Int'l L. (Suppl.) 127-39.

United Nations. Security Council. Official records. Minutes of the emergency session of Jan. 10-11, 1964 on Panama (S/PV.1086)

U.S. Congress. House. Comm. on Foreign Affairs.
> (86.2) Report on United States relations with Panama. Gov't Print. Off. 1960. 89p. (H. rep. no. 2218)
> (86.2) United States relations with Panama. Hearings before the sub-com. on inter-American affairs of the comm. on foreign affairs. . . . Gov't Print. Off. 1960. 107p.

U.S. Congress. House. Comm. on Merchant Marine and Fisheries.
> (85.1) Implementing a treaty and agreement with the Republic of Panama; report to accompany H.R. 6709. Gov't Print. Off. 1957. 12p.
> (85.1) Land transfer under Panama treaty . . . Gov't Print. Off. 1957. 86p.

U.S. Congress. Senate. Comm. on Foreign Relations. The Panama treaty hearings. Ex. F., the treaty of mutual understanding and cooperation, July 15, 18 and 20, 1955. 203p.

—Executive report no. 11. 19p.

U.S. Congress. Senate. Comm. on Interstate and Foreign Commerce.
> (56.1) Hearings . . . on new Panama canal company, the maritime company and the Nicaragua canal company . . . Gov't Print. Off. 1899. 191p.

U.S. Isthmian Canal Commission 1899-1902. . . . Report of the Isthmian canal commission, 1899-1901. Washington, Gov't Print. Off. 1904. 688p.

U.S. Department of State. Diplomatic history of the Panama canal. Correspondence relating to the negotiation and application of certain treaties on the subject of the construction of an interoceanic canal, and accompanying papers. Washington, Gov't Print. Off. 1914. 602p. (53d Cong., 2d Sess. Sen. Doc. 474)

U.S. Department of State Bulletin. Official Releases.
> Agreement with Panama concerning Panama canal. 1955. 32:237-43.
> President signs bill on Canal zone working conditions. 1958. 39: 237-8.

Note from the United States ambassador to the acting minister of foreign relations of Panama, Sept. 17, 1960. 1960. 43:558.

President Kennedy replies to letter from President Chiari of Panama. Dec. 4, 1961. 45:932-3.

Joint communiqué of President Kennedy and President Chiari of Panama, June 13, 1962. 1962. 47:81-2.

Joint communiqué and aide-memoire of representatives of the governments of the Republic of Panama and the United States of America, Jan. 10, 1963. 1963. 48:171.

U.S. and Panama agree on certain procedural matters in canal zone; joint communiqué with U.S. aide-memoire, Jan. 10, 1963. J. F. Kennedy and R. F. Chiari. Feb. 4, 1963. 48:171-3.

U.S. and Panama announce results of canal zone talks; joint communiqué, July 23, 1963. J. F. Kennedy and R. F. Chiari. 49:246-7.

Situation in Panama: White House statements, communiqués, security council debate and exchange of letters, Jan. 10-16, 1964. Feb. 3, 1964. 50:152-6.

President restates U.S. position on Panama and Canal zone statement. Jan. 23, 1964. Feb. 10, 1964. 50:195-6.

O.A.S. council moves to assist in solving U.S.-Panama dispute: statements Jan. 31 and Feb. 4, 1964; with resolutions. Feb. 24, 1964. 50:300-04.

Woolsey, L. H.

Executive agreements relating to Panama. 1943. 37 Am. J. Int'l L. 482-9.

New treaties between the United States and Panama. 1937. 31 Am. J. Int'l L. 297-300.

GENERAL AND HISTORICAL MATERIAL

Alfaro, R. J. and others. Los canales internacionales Panamá. Escuela de Temporado Universidad de Panamá. 1957. 390p.

Ameringer, C. D. Panama canal lobby of Philippe Bunau-Varilla and William Nelson Cromwell. 1963. 68 Am. Hist. Rev. 346-63.

Anguizola, G. A. Fifty years of Isthmian-American relations; an analysis of the causes jeopardizing Isthmian-American friendship. Ann Arbor, University Microfilms. 1954. (Pub. no. 10,139)

Arce, Enrique José. Guía histórica de Panamá. Editorial Nacional. 1942. 240p.

Arias, Harmodio.

El canal de Panamá, un estudio en derecho internacional y diplomacia. Panamá, Editora Panamá América. 1957. 240p.

The Panama Canal. London, King & Son. 1911.

Baty, T. Panama tolls question. 1914. 23 Yale L. J. 389-96.

Baxter, R. R. The law of international waterways with particular regard to interoceanic canals. Cambridge, Harvard Univ. Press. 1964. 371p.

Borland, William P. The permanent government of the canal zone. 1912. 21 Yale L.J. 571-82.

Bullard, Arthur. Panama, the canal, the country, and the people. Rev. ed. New York, Macmillan. 1914. 601p.

Bunau-Varilla, Philippe. Panama, the creation, destruction and resurrection. London. 1913.

Burdick, B. F. The Panama canal and the Canal zone; their character and functions, government and laws. 1937. 3 Fed. B.A.J. 89-92, 104, 123, 127.

de Bustamente, M. Antoine S. Le canal de Panama et le droit international. 1895. 27 Rev. Droit Int'l 112-42.

Chaloner, W. H. The birth of the Panama canal, 1869-1914. 1959. 9 History Today 482-92.

Collins, J. O. Canal zone changes to common law system—long effort to fit civil law code into American system ends. 1934. 20 A.B.A.J. 233-4.

Cox-Sinclair, E. S. The international status of the Panama canal. 1912. 38 Law Mag. & Rev. 1.

Crangle, Roland. Legal aspects of the Panama question. 1904. 12 Am. Law. 214-51.

Curtis, W. J. The history of the purchase by the United States of the Panama canal; the manner of payment; and the distribution of the proceeds of the sale. 1909. 32 Ala. St. B.A. Proc. 129-51.

Dennis, William C. The Panama situation in the light of international law. 1904. 42 Am. L. Register 265.

Díaz, E., Manuel Antonio. La jurisdicción contencioso-administrativa en Panamá. República de Panamá. 1947.

Dimock, Marshall E. Government-operated enterprises in the Panama canal zone. Chicago, Univ. of Chicago Press. 1934. 248p.

Dunn, Russell L. The Panama canal toll and the constitution. 1914. 20 Case & Comment 858-62.

Du Val, Miles Percy.
And the mountains will move; the story of the building of the Panama canal . . . Stanford, Stanford Univ. Press; London, G. Cumberlege, Oxford Univ. Press. 1947. 374p.
Cadiz to Cathay the story of the long diplomatic struggle for the Panama canal. 2d ed. Stanford, Stanford Univ. Press. 1947. 548p.
Isthmian canal policy; an evaluation. Digging the big ditch. Annapolis, U.S. Naval Institute. 1955/56. pp. 263-75, 316-31. (Reprinted from U.S. Naval Institute Proceedings, Vol. 81, no. 3, whole no. 625, March 1955)

Ealy, L. O.
Development of an Anglo-American system of law in the Panama canal zone. 1958. 2 Am. J. Leg. Hist. 283-303.
The republic of Panama in world affairs 1903-1950. Philadelphia, Univ. of Pennsylvania Press. 1951. 207p.
Les Etats-Unis et le canal de Panama. Sept. 8, 1956. 12 Perspectives IV/1-3.

Favell, Thomas Royden. The antecedents of Panama's separation from Colombia; a study in Colombian politics. Medford, Mass. 1950. 8p. (Fletcher School of Law and Diplomacy. Thesis abstract no. 3)

Finch, G. A. Panama-United States claims commission. 1933. 27 Am. J. Int'l L. 750-2.

Fischer, Georges. (Les) relations entre les Etats-Unis et la République de Panama. 1955. 1 Ann. Francais Droit Int'l 85-98.

Fraga Iribaine, Manuel. El canal de Panamá geopolítica diplomacia y derecho internacional. Madrid, Consejo Superior de Investigaciones Científicas, Instituto Francisco de Vitoria, Sección de Derecho Marítimo. 1953. 56p.

Freehoff, Joseph C. America and the canal title; or, an examination, sifting and interpretation of the data bearing on the wresting of the province of Panama from the Republic of Colombia in the Roosevelt administration in 1903 in order to secure title to the canal . . . New York. 1916. 404p.

French, Harold. The ethical value and influence of the Panama canal. 1915. 21 Case & Comment 714-17.

Friedlander, R. A. A reassessment of Roosevelt's role in the Panamanian revolution of 1903. 1961. 14 West. Pol. Q. 535-43.

Garcia-Mora, M. R. International law applicable to the defense of the Panama canal. 1949. 12 U. Det. L.J. 63-73.

Gatell, Frank Otto. The canal in retrospect—some Panamanian and Colombian views. July 1958. 15 (1) The Americas 23-36.

Goethals, George Washington. Government of the canal zone. Princeton, Princeton Univ. Press. 1915. 106p.

Grant, Charles R. The Panama canal and the Monroe doctrine. 1880. 6 So. L. Rev. (n.s.) 729-61.

Gutiérrez Navarro, Carlos. El canal de América: Panamá en la conquista, la colonia, la independencia y la secesión; Atrato-Truandó. Bogotá, Tip. Voto Nacional. 1951. 224p.

Hains, Peter C. Neutralization of the Panama canal. 1909. 3 Am. J. Int'l L. 354-94.

Harding, Earl. The untold story of Panama. New York, Athene Press. 1959. 182p.

Harrigan, A. Needed, a Nicaraguan canal. 1961. 124 World Aff. 52-4.

Hauberg, C. A. Panama: pro mundi beneficio. 1957. 32 Current Hist. 228-36.

Hawes, Herbert B. The recognition of Panama. 1903. 7 Law Notes (N.Y.) 167-9.

Hill, Roscoe R. The Nicaraguan canal idea to 1913. 1948. 28 Hispanic Am. Hist. Rev. 197-211.

History of amendments proposed to the Clayton-Bulwer treaty. Presented by Mr. Root, Jan. 18, 1911. Washington, Gov't Print. Off. 1911. 31p. (61st Cong., 3rd Sess. Sen. Doc. 746)

Howard, Harry N. Military government in the Panama canal zone. Norman, Univ. of Oklahoma Press. 1931. 62p.

Huberich, Charles Henry. The trans-isthmian canal: a study in American diplomatic history. (1825-1904). Austin, Texas. 1904. 31p.

Hunt, B. L. The United States-Panama general claims commission. 1934. 28 Am. J. Int'l L. 61-73.

Hutchinson, Lincoln. The Panama canal and international trade competition. New York, Macmillan. 1915. 283p.

Hyde, Charles Cheney. Recent isthmian canal negotiations. 1901. 10 Yale L.J. 315-21.

"I took the Isthmus." Ex-president Roosevelt's confession, Colombia's protest and editorial comment by American newspapers on "How the United States acquired the right to build the canal." New York. 1911. 108p.

Jiménez, Georgia Isabel. Panama in transition; period of 1849-1940. Ann Arbor, University Microfilms. 1954. (Pub. no. 6640)

Jinesta, Ricardo. El canal de Nicaragua: su historia, base internacional y participación de Costa Rica. San José, Costa Rica, Impr. Nacional. 1958. 92p.

Kaufmann, M. Guillaume. Le loi Americaine du 24 aout 1912 sur le canal de Panama et le droit international. 1912. 14 Rev. Droit Int'l 581-613.

Keasbey, Lindley Miller.
The early diplomatic history of the Nicaragua canal . . . Newark, N.J. The Holbrook Print. Co. 1890. 130p.

The national canal policy (in American Historical Association. Annual report . . . for the year 1902. Washington. 1903. V. 1, pp. 275-88)

The Nicaragua canal and the Monroe doctrine (in Annals of the American Academy of Political & Social Science, 1896, V. VII, no. 1, pp. 1-31)

The Nicaragua canal and the Monroe doctrine; a political history of isthmus transit with special reference to the Nicaragua canal project and the attitude of the United States government . . . New York, G. P. Putnam's Sons. 1896. 622p.

Der Nicaragua-kanal. Geschichte und beurteilung des projekts. . . . Strassburg, N. J. Trubner. 1893. 109p.

The terms and tenor of the Clayton-Bulwer treaty (in Annals of the American Academy of Political & Social Science, 1899. V. XIV, no. 3, pp. 285-309)

Knapp, H. S.
The real status of the Panama canal as regards neutralization. 1910. 4 Am. J. Int'l. 314-58.

Latane, John H. The Panama canal act and the British protest. 1916. 7 Am. J. Int'l L. 17-26.

Lawrence, T. J. The Panama canal and the Clayton-Bulwer treaty (in his essays on some disputed questions in modern international law. Cambridge, Deighton, Bell & Co. 1885, pp. 89-162)

McCain, William David. The United States and the Republic of Panama. . . . Durham, Duke Univ. Press. 1937. 278pp.

Mack, Gerstle. The land divided, a history of the Panama canal and other isthmian canal projects. New York, Knopf. 1944. 650p.

Maity, A. International status of the Panama canal. 1952. 125 Calcutta Rev. 123-33.

Maxey, Edwin.
Legal aspects of the Panama situation. 1903. 13 Yale L.J., 85-9.
The Republic of Panama. 1904. 66 Albany L.J. 14-16.

Miller, Hugh Gordon. The isthmian highway; a review of the problems of the Carribean. New York, Macmillan. 1929. 327p.

Miner, Dwight Carroll. The fight for the Panama route; the story of the Spooner act and the Hay-Herrán treaty. New York, Columbia Univ. Press. 1940. 469p.

Moore, John Bassett. The interoceanic canal and the Hay-Pauncefote treaty. 2 Collected Papers, John B. Moore 253-71.

National Rivers and Harbors Congress. Special Comm. on the Panama Canal. The Panama canal—the sea-level project and national security; a report. Washington, Gov't Print. Off. 1956. 24p. (84th Cong., 2d Sess. House Doc. 446)

Olney, Richard.
Canal tolls legislation and the Hay-Pauncefote treaty. 1913. 6 Law. & Bank. 164.
Fortification of the Panama canal. 1911. 5 Am. J. Int'l L. 398-301.

Oppenheim, Lassa F. L. The Panama canal conflict between Great Britain and the United States of America. Cambridge, Cambridge Univ. Press. 1913. 57p.

Padelford, Norman J.
American rights in the Panama canal. 1940. 34 Am. J. Int'l L. 416-42.
Neutrality, belligerency and the Panama canal. 1941. 35 Am. J. Int'l L. 55-89.
The Panama canal in peace and war. New York, Macmillan. 1942. 327pp.
The Panama canal in time of peace. 1940. 34 Am. J. Int'l L. 601-37.

Parker, F. D. The Central American republics. New York, Oxford Univ. Press. 1964.

Parks, E. Taylor. Colombia and the United States 1765-1934. Durham, Duke Univ. Press. 1935. 554p.

Peirce, Clyde. The Roosevelt Panama libel cases; a factual study of a controversial episode in the career of Teddy Roosevelt, father of the Panama canal. New York, Greenwich Book Pub. 1959. 150p.

Polemica tra Panama e Washington per il canale. 1956. 20 Relaz. Internaz. 1097-98.

Rebolledo, Alvaro. El canal de Panamá; reseña historico-política de la comunicación inter-oceánica, con especial referencia a la separación de Panamá y a los arreglos entre los Estados Unidos y Colombia. Cali, Colombia. 1957. 266p.

The repeal of the provision of the Panama canal act exempting American coastwise vessels from the payment of tolls. (Editorial note) 1914. 8 Am. J. Int'l L. 592-7.

Richards, H. Erle. The Panama canal controversy. Oxford, Clarendon Press. 1913. 48p.

Rivas, Raimundo. Historia diplomática de Colombia (1810-1934). Bogotá, Impr. Nacional. 1961. 812p.

Robbins, A. H. Exemption of Panama canal tolls as affecting the Hay-Pauncefote treaty. 1914. 78 Cent. L.J. 128-9.

Root, Elihu. Addresses on international subjects. Cambridge, Harvard Univ. Press. 1916. (Panama canal, pp. 240-312)

Rowe, Leo S. The work of the joint international commission on Panama claims. 1914. 8 Am. J. Int'l L. 738-57.

Sevareid, Eric. Man who invented Panama. Aug. 1963. 14 American Heritage 106-10.

Smith, George D. The Panama canal. 1912. 7 Ill. L. Rev. 98-118.

Sociedad Panameña de Acción Internacional. Panama-United States relations. A situation that must be changed for the welfare of Panama and the honor of the United States. True hustory of the Panama canal treaty, born from fraud, perfidy, inequity, dishonor, coercion, chicanery, menace, disloyalty and injustice. Panama rights on the Canal zone voiced by distinguished American officials and statesmen. Panama. 1934. 123p.

Spring, Alfred. The recognition of Panama. 1905. 39 Am. L. Rev. 853-70.

Status of the Panama canal Zone. 1956. 106 L.J. 438-70.

Stringfellow, Horace. Panama canal tolls exemption. 1921. 7 A.B.A.J. 305-06.

Svarverud, Carl. The canal crisis. Los Angeles, 1957. 61p.

Taylor, Hannis. The Panama canal; the rule of treaty construction known as *rebus sic stantibus*. 1914. 1 Georgetown L.J. 193-301.

Thompson, Clark W. "Isthmian canal policy of the United States— documentation." Cong. Rec. CI, Pt. 3, March 23, 1955, 3611-16.

Viallate, Achille. Essais d'histoire diplomatique américaine. Le développement territorial des Etats-Unis. Le canal interocéanique. La guerre hispano-américaine. Paris, Librairie Orientale et Americaine E. Guilmoto. 1905. 306p.

Westerman, George W. Fifty years (1903-1953) of treaty negotiations between the United States and Republic of Panama. Panama, Distr. by Panama's Newspaper Guild. 1953. 26p.

White, Harold F. Legal aspects of the Panama canal. 1914. 8 Ill. L. Rev. 442-61.

White, Thomas Raeburn and Tower, Charlemagne. Our duty concerning the Panama canal tolls. Boston, World Peace Foundation. 1913. 16p.

Williams, Mary Wilhelmine. Anglo-American isthmian diplomacy, 1815-1915 . . . Washington, American Historical Association. 1916. 356p.

Wimmer, Karl Ludwig. Die volkerrechtliche stellung des Panamakanals. Munchen. 1959. 133p.

Woolsey, L. H.
Sovereignty of the Panama canal zone. 1926. 20 Am. J. Int'l L. 117-24.

United States-Panama claims commission. 1931. 25 Am. J. Int'l L. 520-3.

THE 1964 PANAMA CRISIS

Alfaro, Ricardo J. Medio siglo de relaciones entre Panamá y los Estados Unidos. Panamá, Impr. Nacional. 1953. 32p.

Allan, Donald A. and Sherman, George. Panama: distrust and delay. Feb. 27, 1964. 30 Reporter 28-9.

America's troubled canal: Panamanians are questioning our sovereignty in the zone. . . . Feb. 1957. Fortune 129-32.

Another "Panama canal": A-blasts may do the job. June 10, 1963. 54 U.S. News 74-5.

Arias, Carlos Arosemena. Emerging Panama: politics and problems (in Wilgus, A. Curtis, ed. The Carribean: the Central American area. 1961, pp. 115-22)

Arias Guardia, Gilberto. Será nuestro; discurso pronunciado ante la asociación Panameña de ingenieros en el ateneo de ciencias y artes el 5 de julio de 1962. Panamá, Dpto. de Relaciones Públicas del Ministerio de Hacienda y Tesoro. 1962. 13p.

Baldwin, Hanson W.
Canal zone's case. N.Y. Times, Feb. 27, 1964, p. 16.

New currents in the Panama canal. N.Y. Times, May 26, 1957, (Magazine), pp. 14-15.

Panama canal's value. N.Y. Times, Jan. 16, 1964, p. 14, col. 5-7.

Ball, George W. A bridge for the Americas. (Address made at a ceremony dedicating the Thatcher Ferry bridge at Balboa Heights, Panama canal zone on Oct. 12, 1962.) 1962. 47 Dep't State Bull. 645-8.

Batista Ballesteros, Isias. El drama de Panamá y América, nuestras relaciones con los E.E.U.U. Panamá, Impr. Panamá. 1961. 175p.

Benitez, Enrique Nrey. The Remon-Eisenhower treaty of 1955. Unpublished master's thesis. George Washington University. 1959.

Biesanz, John Berry. The people of Panama. New York, Columbia Univ. Press. 1955. 418p.

Biesanz, John Berry and Smith, L. M.
Panamanian politics: social factors in Panamanian politics; legal and extra legal patterns in Panamanian government and admin-

istration; parties and power centers: Panamanian nationalism. 1952. 14 J. Pol. 386-402.

Race relations in Panama and the canal zone. July 1951. 57 Am. J. Sociol. 7-14.

Busey, James L. Conflict in Panama: U.S. role in canal zone is complicated by dispute over sovereignty, profits and discrimination in employment. Feb. 15, 1960. 43 New Leader 16-19.

The canal's too small anyway: problem is to find a better one. Jan. 27, 1964. 56 U.S. News 32-3.

Canal Zone. Canal zone code. Orford, N. H., Equity Pub. Co. 1963. 3v.

Castillo Pimentel, Ernesto.
Panamá y los Estados Unidos. Panamá. 1953. 336p.
Política exterior de Panamá; los objetivos de nuestra política exterior, los instrumentos o medios para lograrlos y las bases generales del nuevo tratado que debe la República de Panamá negociar con los Estados Unidos de América. Panamá, Impresora Panamá. 1961. 84p.

Doyle v. Fleming. 219 F. Supp. 277, (D.C.Z. 1963) July 8, 1963. (Doyle flag case)

Les Etats-Unis construiront-ils un nouveau canal trans-océanique pour doubler ou remplacer Panama? 1962. 44 J. Marine Marchande et Navigation Aerienne 1855-6.

Fenwick, Charles G.
Legal aspects of the Panama case. 1964. 58 Am. J. Int'l L. 436-41.
The Organization of American States . . . Washington, D.C. 1963. 601p.

Fiumel, H. Zagadnienie suwerennósii w streifie kanalu Panamskiego. Oct. 1957. 10 Pań i Prawo 641-50.

Flood, D. J. Panama canal zone. Constitutional domain of the United States. 1958. 121 World Aff. 74-7.

Geyelin, Philip. Problems in Panama. Jan. 13, 1964. 163 Wall St. J. 2.

Goldrich, Daniel. Radical nationalism: the political orientations of Panamanian law students. East Lansing, College of Business & Public Service, Bureau of Social & Political Research. 1962. 44p.

Goldrich, Daniel and Scott, E. W. Developing political orientations of Panamanian students. 1961. 23 J. Pol. 84-107.

Goldston, Eli and Devaron, Jose. Latest Panama crisis reflects old tensions: canal tolls assailed. Jan. 21, 1964. 279 J. Commerce 1.
Jan. 22, 1964. 279:1.
Jan. 22, 1964. 279:1.
Jan. 23, 1964. 279:3.
Jan. 24, 1964. 279:3.

Gonionskii, Semen Aleksandrovich. Istoriia panamskoi revolutsii. Moscow, Izd-vo Inta Mezhdunarodnykh Otnosheniy. 1958. 191p.

Gvozdev, Yuri. Panama, the canal and the Yankees. Jan. 22, 1964. New Times (Moscow) 10-12.

Guilfoyle, Joseph M.
Canal controversy: Americans in Panama split with those in canal zone. Feb. 12, 1964. 163 Wall St. J. 8.
Dilemma for Panama. Jan. 22, 1964. 163 Wall St. J. 1.
Panama crisis draws attention to problems of building new canal. Jan. 17, 1964. 163 Wall St. J. 1.

Hunter, Edward. We're asking for it in Panama: why is no American concession to Panamanian demands ever enough? because Communist agents are constantly fomenting hatred of the U.S. March 14, 1959. 6 Nat'l Rev. 583-4.

Izakov, Boris. The Panama events. Jan. 29, 1964. New Times (Moscow) 7-9.

King, H. Thelma. El problema de la soberanía en las relaciones entre Panamá y los Estados Unidos de América. Panamá, Ministerio de Educación. 1961. 274p.

Kuebler, Jeanne. Panama settlement. Feb. 26, 1964. Editorial Research Rep. 143-60.

Lepotier, A.
Le canal de Panama est-il menacé? 1959. 227 Rev. Pol. et Parlementaire 257-68.
Problèmes a Panama? 1957. 13 Rev. de Défense Nat'l 559-71.

Lutz, E. R. Recent arbitration between the United States and Panama. 1934. 2 Fed. B.A.J. 43-7.

Martinez, O. Panama, another Suez? 1960. 198 Contemp. Rev. 548-50, 559.

Martz, John D. Central America, the crisis and the challenge. Chapel Hill, Univ. of North Carolina Press. 1959. 356p.

Meléndez, Próspero. Panamá y el canal; un breve ensayo sobre los problemas que a la nacionalidad panameña ha presentado y sigue presentando la construcción y administración del Canal Panamá. 1961. 25p.

Minger, R. E. Panama, the canal zone and titular sovereignty. 1961. 14 W. Pol. Q. 544-54.

Neumann, William. The Panama canal: America's Suez. March 1957. Liberation 14-16.

O'Brien, R. Barry. A second Panama canal? March 25, 1960. 16 Norwegian Shipping News 287-8.

Okuneva, M. When U.S. imperialism was young. 1962. 8 (10) Int'l Aff. (Moscow) 58-64.

Ortega, Gregorio. Panamá. Habana, Impr. Nacional de Cuba. 1961. 142p.

Padelford, Norman J. The Panama canal and the Suez crisis. 1957. 51 Am. Soc'y Int'l L. Proc. 10-19.

Panama and the U.S.—little troubles grow: there is agitation for more local "sovereignty," a bigger slice of tolls. May 18, 1959. 46 U.S. News 117-18.

Panama—no U.S. backdown. Jan. 27, 1964. 56 U.S. News 29-31.

Parfond, P. Le canal de Suez et le droit international. 1958. Rev. Maritime 528-39.

Perlo, Victor. The dollar over Panama. Feb. 26, 1964. New Times (Moscow) 16-18.

Pizzinelli, C. Panama e il problema del canale. 1960. 14 Comunitá 46-8.

Porras, Demetrio A. Problemas vitales panameños. Panamá, Ministerio de Educación. 1960. 127p.

Proposed canal stirs comment. Feb. 7, 1964. 279 J. Commerce 8.

Ross, Thomas B. Panama and the canal: danger of the new unrest in the Panama canal zone inspired by the recent Cuban revolution of Fidel Castro. July 1959. 2 W. World 19-22.

Schmid, Peter.
Double flags and double standards in Panama. Sept. 30, 1952. Reporter 17-20.
Wetterwolken am Panamakanal. 1952. 4 Monat 389-94.

Sparks, W. Justice and the canal. Feb. 7, 1964. 79 Commonweal 564-6.

Spirin, V. G. and Romanov, L. M. K voprosu o suv erenitete Panamy nad zonoi panamskogo Kanula. July 1962. 32 (7) Sovetskol Gosudarstvo i Pravo 122.

Tate, Mercer D.
The Panama canal and political partnership. 1963. 25 J. Politics 119-38.
Partnerschaft am Panama-kanal? Ursachen und entwicklung der gegensatze swischen Panama und den vereinigten staaten. Jan. 15, 1964. 19 Europa-Archiv 53-64.

Travis, M. B. and Watkins, J. T. Control of the Panama canal; an obsolete shibboleth? 1959. 37 For. Aff. 407-18.

"Truth about Panama." May 2, 1959. New Statesman LVII, p. 598, No. 1468.

Veliz, Claudio. Crisis in Panama. Feb. 1964. 20 World Today 77-83.

Weiner, R. M. Sovereignty of the Panama isthmus. 1960. 16 Intra. L. Rev. 65-77.

What the squabble in Panama is all about: interview with representative Armistead I. Selden, jr., chairman of inter-American affairs. Jan. 27, 1964. 56 U.S. News 34-7.

Why Panama canal isn't going the way of Suez: it's U.S. property, with zone nailed down by perpetual lease. Aug. 17, 1956. U.S. News 54-5.

Why Panama errupted: Castro tactics spark anti-U.S. violence. Jan. 20, 1964. 56 U.S. News 32-3.

Woolsey, Theodore S. The recognition of Panama and its results. 3 Can. L. Rev. 91-101.

SUPPLEMENT

L'affaire de Panama peut-elle devenir, dur point de vue de la marine marchande, une nouvelle affaire de Suez? Jan. 16, 1964. 46 J. Marine Marchande et Navigation Aérienne 107-9.

Benedetti, E.   Problema de la soberanía en la zona del canal. 1961/62. 5 Anuario de Derecho (Panamá) 239.

Bunau-Varilla, Philippe.   Historia auténtica de la escandalosa negociación del tratado del canal de Panamá escrita por el propio autor de esa convención. 2d ed. Panamá, Impreso en los Talleres Impresora. 1964. 102p.

Bunker, Ellsworth.   OAS council moves to assist in solving U.S.-Panama dispute. Feb. 24, 1964. 50 Dep't State Bull. 300-04.

China backs up Panama. Jan. 17, 1964. 7 Peking Rev. 6-8.

Cordero Torres, J. M. El status internacional del canal de Panamá. Jan/Feb. 1964. Revista Política Internacional 275-345.

Dubois, Jules.   Danger over Panama. Indianapolis, Bobbs-Merrill. 1964. 409p.

Finney, J. W.   A second canal? March 28, 1964. 150 New Republic 212-14.

Fox, D. J.
The future of the Panama canal. Sept. 1964. 45 Dock & Harbour Authority 143-45.
Prospects for the Panama canal. Dec. 1963. 53 Ass'n Am. Geog. Ann. 590.

Geyelin, P.   The irksome Panama wrangle. April 9, 1964. 30 Reporter 14-17.

Ikonikoff, M.   Les raisons d'un conflict—quand les Etats-Unis créaient l'état de Panama. March 1964. Croissance de Jeunes Nations 10-12.

International Commission of Jurists.   Investigating Comm. Report on the events in Panama. Jan. 9-12, 1964. 46p.

Johnson, Lyndon B.   U.S. plans new sea-level canal and new treaty on existing canal: statement. Jan. 4, 1965. 52 Dep't State Bull. 5-6.

Die kirche und die Panama-krise. Feb. 15, 1964. 28 Orientierung 33-35.

McDowell, E.   Will we lose the canal? Feb. 11, 1964. 16 Nat'l Rev. 107-8.

Metford, J. C. J.   The background to Panama. April 1964. 40 Int'l Aff. (London) 277-86.

Panama Canal Information Office.   The Panama canal: fiftieth Anniversary; the story of a great conquest. 1964. 122p.

Quimbaya, Anteo.   Problemas históricos de actualidad; por qué el canal de Panamá debe ser y será de los panameños? 2 ed. Bogotá. Ediciones Suramérica. 1964. 206p.

Rippy, J. F.   United States and Panama; the high cost of appeasement. Spring 1964. 17 Inter-Am. Econ. Aff. 87-94.

Santis, S. de.   La controversia del canale di Panama. Feb. 1964. 18 Comunità 29-36.

Tanner, James C.   New U.S. canal policy may not give Panama benefits once expected . . . Jan. 15, 1965. 165 Wall St. J. 1.

NOTES
TO
THE WORKING PAPER ON THE PANAMA CANAL

[1] Inter-American Treaty of Reciprocal Assistance, opened for signature at Rio de Janeiro, Sept. 2, 1947, 62 Stat. 1681, T.I.A.S. No. 1838, 21 U.N.T.S. 79. This Panamanian invocation of articles 6 and 9(a) of the Rio Pact directly raised a grave charge of United States "aggression"; it was the first time that the United States has been accused as an aggressor under the Rio de Janeiro Treaty. See N.Y. Times, Jan 11, 1964, p. 5, col. 1.

[2] 59 Stat. 1031, T.S. No. 993. Article 34 authorizes the Security Council to investigate any dispute or situation "which might lead to international friction or give rise to a dispute." Article 35 authorizes any member of the United Nations to bring such a dispute to the Security Council. The Council did meet in emergency session on the night of January 10, and it agreed by consensus to appeal to the United States and Panama for an immediate cease fire. U.N. SECURITY COUNCIL OFF. REC. 19th year, 1086th meeting (S/PV.1086) (1964).

[3] The Inter-American Peace Committee was created pursuant to Resolution XIV of the Second Meeting of Consultation of Foreign Ministers at Havana in 1940, which recommended that the Governing Board of the Pan American Union:

> "organize, in the American capital deemed most suitable for the purpose, a committee composed of representatives of five countries, which shall have the duty of keeping constant vigilance to insure that States between which any dispute exists or may arise, of any nature whatsoever, may solve it as quickly as possible, and of suggesting, without detriment to the methods adopted by the parties or to the procedures which they may agree upon, the measures and steps which may be conducive to a settlement." (In *International Conferences of American States, First Supplement 1933-1940*, at 360 (1940).)

Since its installation in 1948 the Inter-American Peace Committee has functioned very successfully as a mediator in a number of Inter-American disputes. It is a body with considerable autonomous powers to mediate in such disputes without requiring specific authority from the O.A.S. Council; it can perform also as an informal commission of investigation and conciliation without being obliged to follow the fairly rigid procedures for peaceful settlement of disputes established in existing American treaties. See generally FENWICK, THE ORGANIZATION OF AMERICAN STATES 106-09, 198-208 (1963).

[4] Venezuela, the Dominican Republic, Argentina, Colombia, and Chile, Chile having been appointed to the Peace Committee on this occasion by the O.A.S. Council to substitute for the United States.

[5] Panama had excepted United States A.I.D. personnel and the Peace Corps from those U.S. officials asked to leave on January 17, and President Chiari had expressed the hope that there would be no break in the continuity of Alliance for Progress programs in Panama despite the diplomatic breach with the United States. Nevertheless Panama received no economic assistance from the United States during the interruption in relations; the United States explained that the suspension of aid was done not for political purposes but for purely practical reasons because its administering personnel had had to leave Panama. N.Y. Times, Jan. 22, 1964, p. 1, col. 2. *But see* N.Y. Times, Jan. 18, 1964, p. 2, col. 7, reporting a difference of opinion between American officials whether the United States had "ordered" or "suggested" that its A.I.D. personnel leave Panama.

[6] Inter-American Treaty of Reciprocal Assistance, opened for signature at Rio de Janeiro, Sept. 2, 1947, 62 Stat. 1681, T.I.A.S. No. 1838, 21 U.N.T.S. 79.

[7] Article 11.

[8] See FENWICK, THE ORGANIZATION OF AMERICAN STATES 93-94, 236-46 (1963).

[9] The O.A.S. resolutions of February 4 and 7, 1964 are printed in 50 DEP'T STATE BULL. 304 (1964).

[10] N.Y. Times, Feb. 17, 1964, p. 1, col. 5. In March another factual investigation was held in Panama by a committee of the International Commission of Jurists at the request of the Panamanian Bar Association. The Panamanian Bar Association charged that the United States, by the conduct of her troops during the January rioting, had violated articles 3, 5, and 20(1) of the Universal Declaration of Human Rights—the right to life, liberty, and security of person; the right not to be subjected to torture or to cruel, inhuman or degrading treatment or punishment; and the right to freedom of peaceful assembly and association. *Id.*, March 1, 1964, p. 31, col. 2; March 15, 1964, p. 28, col. 1. The Jurists' Investigating Committee conducted hearings in Panama at which representatives of Panama and the United States presented testimonial and documentary evidence and were able to question witnesses. (Transcript of Proceedings on file in Library of the Association of the Bar of the City of New York.) On June 10, 1964 the Committee published its Report (reported herein as Appendix, beginning at page 60), which exonerated the United States of all charges of violating the Universal Declaration of Human Rights and strongly criticized the Government of Panama for failing for four days to take any action to quell the rioting. But the Committee was also critical of United States citizens living in the Canal Zone who "have developed a particular state of mind not conducive to the promotion of happier relations between them and the people of Panama."

[11] N.Y. Times, April 4, 1964, p. 2, col. 4.

[12] A thorough study of early canal projects up to De Lesseps' attempt is to be found in DU VAL, CADIZ TO CATHAY: THE STORY OF THE LONG DIPLOMATIC STRUGGLE FOR THE PANAMA CANAL (2d ed. 1947).

[13] PADELFORD, THE PANAMA CANAL IN PEACE AND WAR 4 (1942).

[14] 20 CONG. REC. 338 (1889), quoted in PADELFORD, *op. cit. supra* note 13, at 14.

[15] *E.g.*, Travis & Watkins, *Control of the Panama Canal: An Obsolete Shibboleth?*, 37 FOREIGN AFFAIRS 407 (1959). *But see* Baldwin, *Panama Canal's Value*, N.Y. Times, Jan. 16, 1964, p. 14, col. 7.

[16] See the remarks of Adm. James S. Russell, then Vice Chief of Naval Operations, on February 2, 1960 in *Hearings on United States Relations With Panama Before the Subcommittee on Inter-American Affairs of the House Committee on Foreign Affairs*, 86th Cong., 2d Sess. 101 (1960).

[17] See pp. 42-43 *infra*.

[18] UNITED ARAB REPUBLIC, SUEZ CANAL AUTHORITY, MONTHLY REPORT, Jan. 1964, at 3.

[19] *Ibid.* "Net tonnage" is the calculated cargo capacity of a vessel, in contrast to "cargo tonnage", which is the actual weight in long tons of the cargo transported.

[20] Statement of Secretary of State Dulles at the Suez Conference, Aug. 16, 1956, in THE SUEZ CANAL PROBLEM: JULY 26-SEPTEMBER 22, 1956, at 73 (Dept's State Pub. 6392) (1956).

[21] ANNUAL REPORT OF THE PANAMA CANAL COMPANY AND THE CANAL ZONE GOVERNMENT FOR THE FISCAL YEAR 1962, at 5 (1962).

[22] *Id.* at 11.

[23] 10,900,843 net vessel tons, Panama Canal measurement, out of a total of 65,378,845 net vessel tons, *id.* at 57.

[24] *Ibid.* In view of the current tendency to place vessels under flags of convenience provided by certain smaller countries like Liberia and Panama, in order to avoid the impact of tax and labor laws, it may well be that United States ship-owners making use of the Panama Canal are an even larger group than statistics based on the flag of vessels would indicate.

[25] They are, in rank of net vessel tonnage (Panama Canal measurement) moving over them: (1) East coast United States—Asia, cargo movements to and from Japan accounting for 76.9 per cent of the cargo flow over this route; (2) east coast United States—west coast South America, the bulk of the cargo flow being movement of raw materials from South America to the industrial complex of the United States; (3) Europe—west coast South America, Atlantic-bound raw materials being the main contributors to cargo movements over this route; (4) Europe—west coast United States and Canada; (5) United States inter-coastal, including Alaska and Hawaii; (6) Europe —Oceania, cargo flowing principally between New Zealand and Great

Britain; (7) east coast South America—west coast United States, the cargo movement consisting almost entirely of a flow of petroleum products from Venezuela to the United States; and (8) West Indies—Asia, about 75 per cent of the total cargo flow being Cuban sugar bound for China, Japan, and Russia. *Id.* at 7-10.

[26] 42,035,000 long tons out of a total of 67,525,000 long tons, *id.* at 7.

[27] A detailed analysis of the types of interest in international waterways—those of the users, the territorial sovereign, and the operator or supervisor of the waterway—is to be found in BAXTER, THE LAW OF INTERNATIONAL WATERWAYS 21-37 (1964).

[28] Panamanian reaction was reportedly bitter to an announcement on April 16, 1964 by U.S. President Johnson that the United States and Colombia had agreed to begin an immediate study of the feasibility of a sea-level canal to be cut through Colombian territory. N.Y. Times, April 18, 1964, p. 10, col. 3.

[29] Reported in Baldwin, *Canal Zone's Case,* N.Y. Times, Feb. 27, 1964, p. 16, col. 4.

[30] *Ibid.*

[31] The Canal Zone Government paid 1,173 full-time employees at U.S. citizen rates and 1,297 full-time employees at non-U.S. citizen rates. ANNUAL REPORT OF THE PANAMA CANAL COMPANY AND THE CANAL ZONE GOVERNMENT FOR THE FISCAL YEAR 1962, at 137 (1962).

[32] The Panama Canal Company paid 2,574 full-time employees at U.S. citizen rates and 8,673 full-time employees at non-U.S. citizen rates. *Id.* at 103-04.

[*] Most of this subsection has been extracted, without change save condensation, from BAXTER, THE LAW OF INTERNATIONAL WATERWAYS, © 1964 by the President and Fellows of Harvard College. The Association is grateful to the publisher, the Harvard University Press, for permission to reproduce this material.

[33] Convention between the United States of America and the Republic of Panama for the Construction of a Ship Canal to Connect the Waters of the Atlantic and Pacific Oceans, signed at Washington, Nov. 18, 1903, 33 Stat. 2234, T.S. No. 431.

[34] DU VAL, CADIZ TO CATHAY: THE STORY OF THE LONG DIPLOMATIC STRUGGLE FOR THE PANAMA CANAL 380 (2d ed. 1947).

[35] Convention between Germany and China respecting the Lease of Kiaochow, signed at Peking, March 6, 1898, sec. I, art. III, 1 MACMURRAY, TREATIES AND AGREEMENTS WITH AND CONCERNING CHINA, 1894-1919, at 112 (1921).

[36] Convention between France and China for the Lease of Kuang-chou Wan, signed at Peking, May 27, 1898, arts. I and III, 1 MAC-MURRAY, *op. cit. supra* note 35, at 128; Convention between Russia and China for the Lease of the Liaotung Peninsula, signed at Peking, March 27, 1898, arts. I and II, *id.* at 119.

[37] *E.g.,* De Pouvourville, *Les Fictions internationales en Extrême-*

Orient, 6 REVUE GÉNÉRALE DE DROIT INTERNATIONAL PUBLIC 113, 118 (1899) ; 2 MÉRIGNHAC, TRAITÉ DE DROIT PUBLIC INTERNATIONAL 488 (1907).

38 Memorandum of the Solicitor of the Department of State, inclosure to Secretary of State Hay to Mr. Conger, Feb. 3, 1900, [1900] FOREIGN REL. U.S. 387, 389 (1902) ; the views of the authorities are extensively discussed in NOREM, KIAOCHOW LEASED TERRITORY 55-86 (1936).

39 Secretary of State Hay to Mr. de Abaldía, the Panamanian Minister, Oct. 24, 1904, [1904] FOREIGN REL. U.S. 613, 615 (1905).

40 General Treaty of Friendship and Cooperation between the United States of America and Panama, signed at Washington, March 2, 1936, art. III, para. 6, 53 Stat. 1807, T.S. No. 945. The provision related to the landing of passengers and cargo in the area so defined.

41 Note from the United States Ambassador to the Acting Minister of Foreign Relations of Panama, Sept. 17, 1960, 43 DEP'T STATE BULL. 558 (1960). There had been considerable opposition in the Congress to the flying of the Panamanian flag, and the expenditure of funds for the erection of a pole to fly that flag had been forbidden by section 201 of the Department of Commerce Appropriation Act for 1961, 74 Stat. 93. See also *Hearings on United States Relations with Panama Before the Subcommittee on Inter-American Affairs of the House Committee on Foreign Affairs,* 86th Cong., 2d Sess. (1960), which are very largely devoted to a consideration of this issue.

42 Joint Communiqué of President Kennedy and President Chiari of Panama, June 13, 1962, 48 DEP'T STATE BULL. 81 (1962) ; Address of Under Secretary of State Ball at Dedication of Thatcher Ferry Bridge, Balboa Heights, C.Z., Oct. 12, 1962, *id.* at 645, 648; Joint Communiqué and Aide-Memoire of Representatives of the Governments of the Republic of Panama and the United States of America, Jan. 10, 1963, 48 *id.* 171 (1963). The "Doyle flag case," Doyle v. Fleming, 219 F.Supp. 277 (D.C.Z. 1963), was instituted when on October 12, 1962 the Panamanian and United States flags were flown at equal heights from separate flag poles on the Thatcher Ferry Bridge. The plaintiff's prayer that Canal Zone Governor Fleming be enjoined from displaying any flag but the United States flag in the Canal Zone was denied.

43 Mr. de Obaldía to Secretary of State Hay, Aug. 11, 1904, [1904] FOREIGN REL. U.S. 598, 599 (1905). The reference in this note to the respective positions of the Republic of Panama and of the United States as those of "lessor and lessee" (at 600) further link the Treaty of 1903 with the international leases of that period.

44 Declaration of the Panamanian Academy of International Law on the Suez and Panama Canals, Jan. 1957; the same contention is made in a letter from Sr. Roberto F. Arias, the Ambassador of Panama, to The Times (London), May 1, 1957, p. 11, col. 5.

45 Order of the Secretary of War, June 24, 1904, in EXECUTIVE

ORDERS RELATING TO THE PANAMA CANAL 26 (1922), and [1904] FOREIGN REL. U.S. 586 1905). The first protest by the Panamanian Government was reported to the Department of State on July 25. [1904] FOREIGN REL. U.S. 586 (1905).

[46] Memorandum by the Secretary of State of a Conversation with the Panamanian Minister (Alfaro), Dec. 15, 1923, [1923] 2 FOREIGN REL. U.S. 682 (1938).

[47] Article VII.

[48] General Treaty of Friendship and Cooperation, *supra* note 40, arts. II and VI.

[49] Treaty cited *supra* note 33, art. VII, para. 3. Concerning the diplomatic history of the right of intervention secured by the Treaty, see PADELFORD, THE PANAMA CANAL IN PEACE AND WAR 60-63 (1942). The right was renounced by the United States in the Treaty of 1936, *supra* note 40, art. VI.

[50] Treaty cited *supra* note 33, art. VII, para. 2. The right was renounced by the United States in the Treaty of Mutual Understanding and Cooperation between the United States of America and the Republic of Panama, signed at Panama, Jan. 25, 1955, art. IV, 6 U.S.T. 2273, T.I.A.S. No. 3297, 243 U.N.T.S. 211.

[51] Treaty cited *supra* note 33, arts. V and VIII.

[52] Treaty of 1936, *supra* note 40, art. VIII; and see Convention between the United States of America and the Republic of Panama regarding the Colón Corridor and Certain Other Corridors Through the Canal Zone, signed at Panamá, May 24, 1950, 6 U.S.T. 461, T.I.A.S. No. 3180, 241 U.N.T.S. 139.

[53] Treaty cited *supra* note 52, art. IV.

[54] Treaty of 1955, *supra* note 50, art. XII.

[55] Treaty of 1936, *supra* note 40, art. III, para. 2, which in general excludes from residence in the Canal Zone persons other than employees of the United States Government; members of the United States Armed Forces; contractors' employees; employees of companies doing business in the Zone; persons engaged in religious, educational, and similar work; their families; and their servants.

[56] Treaty of 1936, *supra* note 40, art. V.

[57] Treaty between the United States and Panama for the Mutual Extradition of Criminals, signed at Panamá, May 25, 1904, 34 Stat. 2851, T.S. No. 445.

[58] Cited *supra* note 33.

[59] PADELFORD, THE PANAMA CANAL IN PEACE AND WAR 75 (1942).

[60] Agreement Authorizing Panamanian Nautical Inspectors to Board Vessels of Panamanian Registry in the Canal Zone for the Purpose of Ascertaining Compliance with Panamanian Maritime and Labor Laws, signed at Panamá, Aug. 5, 1957, 8 U.S.T. 1413, T.I.A.S. No. 3893.

[61] A term characterized by Lord McNair as "inclined to raise the blood pressure of the person who uses it." *Treaties and Sovereignty*, in SYMBOLAE VERZIJL 222, 226 (1958).

[62] U.S. Const. art. IV, §3, and art. I, §8; New York ex rel. Rogers v. Graves, 299 U.S. 401 (1937). See PADELFORD, THE PANAMA CANAL IN PEACE AND WAR 184 (1942).

[63] Act of June 28, 1902, 32 Stat. 481.

[64] Act of Aug. 24, 1912, 37 Stat. 560.

[65] See generally PADELFORD, *op. cit. supra* note 62, at 183-259.

[66] Act of Sept. 26, 1950, 64 Stat. 1038, codified in scattered sections of 2 C.Z.C. (1962).

[67] Act of June 29, 1948, §2, 62 Stat. 1076, as amended by Act of Sept. 26, 1950, §§5-10, 64 Stat. 1042, now 2 C.Z.C. §§61-68 (1962).

[68] 2 C.Z.C. §63 (1962).

[69] PADELFORD, *op. cit. supra* note 62, at 197-98.

[70] 2 C.Z.C. §64 (1962).

[71] ANNUAL REPORT OF THE PANAMA CANAL COMPANY AND THE CANAL ZONE GOVERNMENT FOR THE FISCAL YEAR 1962, at 12-28 (1962).

[72] 2 C.Z.C. §31 (1962).

[73] Burdick, *The Panama Canal and the Canal Zone: Their Character, Functions, Government and Laws,* 3 FED. B.J. 89, 91 (1937); see 2 C.Z.C. §2 (1962).

[74] Public education in the Canal Zone is divided between two school systems with differing curricula: For U.S. citizens there are schools through junior college conducted in English; for pupils of Latin American nationalities there are schools through senior high school conducted in Spanish. ANNUAL REPORT OF THE PANAMA CANAL COMPANY AND THE CANAL ZONE GOVERNMENT FOR THE FISCAL YEAR 1962, at 115-16 (1962).

[75] *Id.* at 105-38.

[76] A new Canal Zone Code was enacted by the Congress and approved by the President on October 18, 1962. 76A Stat. 1.

[77] 18 U.S.C. §5 expressly excludes the Canal Zone from the territorial application of title 18.

[78] *E.g.,* Act of Feb. 16, 1933, §1, 47 Stat. 812, now 2 C.Z.C. §1131 (1962), making the laws and regulations governing the postal service of the United States applicable to the postal service of the Canal Zone.

[79] *E.g.,* Act of July 18, 1956, §201, 70 Stat. 572, as amended, 18 U.S.C. §1401, relating to narcotics.

[80] *E.g.,* statutes relating to employment by the Federal Government.

[81] Huasteca Petroleum Co. v. United States, 14 F.2d 495 (E.D.N.Y. 1926) (taking of depositions); Panama Agencies Co. v. Franco, 111 F.2d 263 (5th Cir. 1940) (Merchant Marine Act).

[82] See 35 C.F.R. §§6, 10. The implied powers of the President in this respect were upheld in McConaughey v. Morrow, 263 U.S. 39 (1923).

[83] 3 C.Z.C. §§171, 172 (1962).

[84] 3 C.Z.C. §1 (1962).

[85] 3 C.Z.C. §141 (1962).

[86] PADELFORD, *op. cit. supra* note 62, at 195.

[87] Act of Aug. 24, 1912, §13, 37 Stat. 569, now 2 C.Z.C. §34 (1962).

[88] Exec. Order No. 10398, Sept. 26, 1952, 17 Fed. Reg. 8647 (1952).

[89] PADELFORD, *op. cit. supra* note 62, at 261-62.

[90] The original basic toll rate prescribed by the President in 1912 for laden vessels was $1.20 per net vessel-ton. But language used in the Panama Canal Act of 1912 required consideration of the tonnage of a vessel under United States rules of measurement as well as under the newly developed Panama Canal rules of measurement when computing tolls, and this dual system of measurement enabled ship-owners to reduce the basis for their toll payments with the result that the prescribed $1.20 rate actually became fictional, and the rate shipowners were in fact paying decreased to about 87.04 cents in 1936. The Act of Aug. 24, 1937, 50 Stat. 750, pursuant to which the President changed the toll rate to 90 cents, abolished the dual system of measurement. PADELFORD, *op. cit. supra* note 62, 111-17.

[91] See *Hearing on H.R. 8677 Before a Subcommittee of the Senate Committee on Armed Services,* 81st Cong., 2d Sess. 7, 17 (1950).

[92] 64 Stat. 1038, codified in scattered sections of 2 C.Z.C. (1962).

[93] 2 C.Z.C. §§62, 412, (b), (c), (e) (1962).

[94] § 12, 64 Stat. 1043, now 2 C.Z.C. §412 (b) (1962).

[95] S. REP. No. 2531, 81st Cong., 2d Sess. 4 (1950); *Hearing on H.R. 8677 Before a Subcommittee of the Senate Committee on Armed Services,* 81st Cong., 2d Sess. at 7 (1950).

[96] 2 C.Z.C. §70 (1962); concerning the dividends of $15,000,000 paid for fiscal years 1955 and 1956, see FOURTH ANNUAL REPORTS OF THE PANAMA CANAL COMPANY AND THE CANAL ZONE GOVERNMENT, 1955, at 5 (1956); and FIFTH ANNUAL REPORTS, 1956, at 5 (1957). The Act of Aug. 25, 1959, 73 Stat. 428, provided that $10,000,000 of retained revenues were to be deemed to be paid into the Treasury as a dividend, and the Canal Company was in turn empowered to borrow up to an equivalent amount from the Treasury. 2 C.Z.C. §71 (1962).

[97] In addition to the amounts which are mentioned in note 96 *supra,* a total of $23,994,905 has been paid as dividends prior to June 30, 1951. ANNUAL REPORT OF THE PANAMA CANAL COMPANY AND THE CANAL ZONE GOVERNMENT FOR THE FISCAL YEAR 1958, at 50 (1959).

[98] ANNUAL REPORT OF THE PANAMA CANAL COMPANY AND THE CANAL ZONE GOVERNMENT FOR THE FISCAL YEAR 1962, at 48 (1962).

[99] Grace Line, Inc. v. Panama Canal Co., 143 F. Supp. 539 (S.D.N.Y. 1956), rev'd, 243 F. 2d 844 (2d Cir. 1957), rev'd, 356 U.S. 309 (1958).

[100] *Report on Audit of Panama Canal Company and the Canal Zone Government for the Fiscal Year Ended June 30, 1954,* H. Doc. No. 160, 84th Cong., 1st Sess. 2-3 (1955), quoted in Grace Line, Inc. v. Panama Canal Co., 243 F.2d 844, 847 (2d Cir. 1957).

[101] Panama Canal Co. v. Grace Line, Inc., 356 U.S. 309 (1958), Brief for Grace Line, p. 44.

[102] Panama Canal Co. v. Grace Line, Inc. 356 U.S. 309 (1958), Brief for the Panama Canal Company, p. 21, n. 49.

[103] Panama Canal Co. v. Grace Line, Inc., 356 U.S. 309, 317 (1958).

[104] See Revisers' Note, *History*, 2 C.Z.C. §412 (1962).

[105] Convention between the United States of America and the Republic of Panama for the Construction of a Ship Canal to Connect the Waters of the Atlantic and Pacific Oceans, signed at Washington, Nov. 18, 1903, art. XIV, 33 Stat. 2234, T.S. No. 431.

[106] General Treaty of Friendship and Cooperation between the United States of America and Panama, signed at Washington, March 2, 1936, art. VII, 53 Stat. 1807, T.S. No. 945.

[107] Explanatory Statement accompanying message from the President to the Senate, May 9, 1955, in *Hearings on the Panama Treaty before the Senate Committee on Foreign Relations*, 84th Cong., 1st Sess. 4 (1955).

[108] Treaty of Mutual Understanding and Cooperation between the United States of America and the Republic of Panama, signed at Panamá, Jan. 25, 1955, art. I, 6 U.S.T. 2273, T.I.A.S. No. 3297, 243 U.N.T.S. 211. The $1,500,000 increase in the annuity to Panama is provided by annual appropriations from the Treasury for the Department of State, and the basic $430,000 is considered an operating expense of the Canal and is furnished out of tolls revenues. See ANNUAL REPORT OF THE PANAMA CANAL COMPANY AND THE CANAL ZONE GOVERNMENT FOR THE FISCAL YEAR 1962, at 50 (1962); 2 C.Z.C. §62 (g) (1) (1962).

[109] Declaration of the Panamanian Academy of International Law on the Suez and Panama Canals, Jan. 31, 1957.

[110] PADELFORD, THE PANAMA CANAL IN PEACE AND WAR 240 (1942).

[111] Kennedy, *Bitterness of Panama Grievances Stands in Way of Reconciliation*, N.Y. Times, Jan. 18, 1964, p. 3, col. 1.

[112] *Hearings on the Panama Treaty before the Senate Committee on Foreign Relations*, 84th Cong., 1st Sess. 11 (1955).

[113] Memorandum of Understandings Reached, Item 1, Annexed to Treaty of Mutual Understanding and Cooperation, *supra* note 108.

[114] ANNUAL REPORT OF THE PANAMA CANAL COMPANY AND THE CANAL ZONE GOVERNMENT FOR THE FISCAL YEAR 1962, at 36 (1962).

[115] In 1960, in response to Panamanian complaints, President Eisenhower proposed a program which would give Panamanians greater access to skilled and supervisory positions, 42 DEP'T STATE BULL. 798 (1960). Yet two years later, when Panamanian President Chiari visited the United States, equal employment opportunities were still an issue, 47 *id.* 81 (1962).

[116] ANNUAL REPORT OF THE PANAMA CANAL COMPANY AND THE CANAL ZONE GOVERNMENT FOR THE FISCAL YEAR 1962, at 37 (1962).

[117] DU VAL, AND THE MOUNTAINS WILL MOVE 142 (1947).

[118] PADELFORD, *op. cit. supra* note 110, at 221-25, 54-55.

[119] *Id.* at 219.

[120] Treaty cited *supra* note 106, art. III.

[121] Treaty cited *supra* note 108, art. XII.

[122] Exchange of Notes, annexed to Treaty of 1936 cited *supra* note 106.

[123] Memorandum of Understanding Reached, Item 4, annexed to Treaty of 1955, cited *supra* note 108.

[124] Treaty cited *supra* note 108, art. V.

[125] Memorandum of Understandings Reached, Items 7, 8, and 9, annexed to Treaty cited *supra* note 108.

[126] ANNUAL REPORT OF THE PANAMA CANAL COMPANY AND THE CANAL ZONE GOVERNMENT FOR THE FISCAL YEAR 1962, at 21, 22 (1962).

[127] Joint Communiqué, June 13, 1962, 47 DEP'T STATE BULL. 81 (1962).

[128] Note from the United States Ambassador to the Acting Minister of Foreign Relations of Panama, Sept. 17, 1960, 43 DEP'T STATE BULL. 558 (1960).

[129] Joint Communiqué and Aide-Mémoire de Representatives of the Governments of the Republic of Panama and the United States of America, Jan. 10, 1963, 48 *id.* 171 (1963).

[130] Joint Communiqué and Aide-Mémoire, cited *supra* note 129.

against the Governor of the Canal Zone.[131]

[131] Doyle v. Fleming, 219 F.Supp. 277 (D.C.Z. 1963). The Zonian's petition for an injunction was denied. However, United States stamps continue to be used in the Canal Zone.

[132] N.Y. Times, May 5, 1964, p. 1, col. 7.

[133] N.Y. Times, Jan. 19, 1964, p. 25, cols. 4, 8.

[134] TRUMAN, YEAR OF DECISIONS 377 (1955). See also Radio Address of President Truman, Aug. 9, 1945, 13 DEP'T STATE BULL. ___, 212 ___ 45). At the time of the Suez Canal crisis, when a que___ was ___sed whether President Truman had indeed suggested ___ the ___nama Canal be internationalized, Secretary of State Dull___ ___plied ___ at a careful search of the Department of State records h___ ___ncov-___d no such offer. News Conference Statement by Secreta___ ___ State ___es, Aug. 28, 1956, in THE SUEZ CANAL PROBLEM, JULY ___ ___TEM-___2, 1956, at 295, 298 (Dep't State Pub. 6392) (1956).

___ *Report to the Senate Foreign Relations Committee,* 8___ ___ong., ___ ss. 15 (1960).

___ ___.Y. Times, Aug. 21, 1956, p. 4, col. 5.

___ ___ldwin, *The Panama Canal,* N.Y. Times, Aug. 12, ___ p. 3, ___ ___nd Aug. 13, 1960, p. 31, vol 1.

___ ___ice of America radio interview, Feb. 14, 1964, 50 I___ ___TATE ___ 330, 335 (1964).

___ N.Y. Times, April 17, 1964, p. 1, col. 2.

___ N.Y. Times, Jan. 21, 1964, p. 10, col. 4.

___ *bid.*

___ *bid.*